ARCHITECT'S GUIDE TO
ROME

Architecture and Gardens: Pius IV's casina in the Vatican gardens, the work of Pirro Ligorio (c.f. no. 57).

ARCHITECT'S GUIDE TO
ROME

RENZO SALVADORI

Butterworth Architecture

London   Boston   Singapore   Sydney   Toronto   Wellington

First published in Great Britain in 1990
by Butterworth Architecture
an imprint of Butterworth Scientific

 PART OF REED INTERNATIONAL P.L.C.

Translated by Brenda Balich

© Renzo Salvadori, Canal Libri, Venice
ISBN 0 408 50054 9

Printed in Italy
Stamperia di Venezia, Venice
126-89

Contents

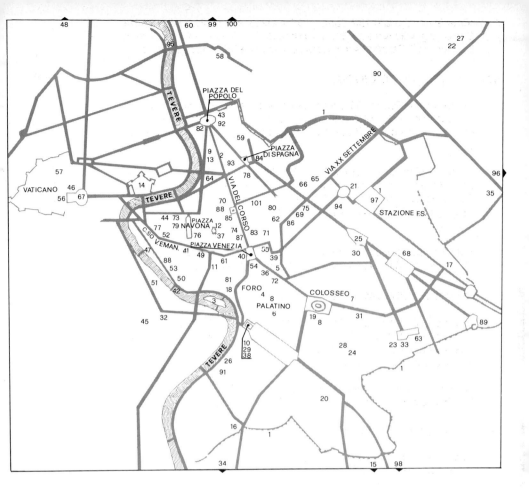

Rome map. Figures refer to item numbers.

A view of antiquity. From «Antichità di Roma» by G.B. Piranesi (1756).

FOREWORD

Butterworth Architecture intend this series of Architect's Guides to provide architects (and all those primarily interested in architecture) with a compact historical summary and description of over a hundred buildings in each city selected. The guides accordingly cover the fullest possible historical range, but unlike tourist guides describe buildings in full depth of architectural detail, as well as including a comprehensive section, in every case, on twentieth-century architecture up to the present day. In addition every guide contains a description of a key design element characteristic of each city, not so much a building as a metaphor for that city. For Rome, the author found the fountains exemplary both from a historical and an artistic point of view.

In the late twentieth century urban planning and design has become a subject of key importance to all cities, and each city demonstrates its own historic solutions, as well as their related problems and the way in which these are being solved. A city is not only a collection of buildings: it has its own special environment, often more precious and fragile than the individual buildings which created it.

The urban setting of Rome is dealt with here in some detail in view of its unique development over twenty centuries.

This volume being nonetheless a particular selection reflects the personal taste, and prejudices too of the author. In the text this is balanced, and enhanced perhaps, by some of the best known authorities on Italian architecture, whose works the reader may further refer (see Bibliography).

Finally, since we are dealing with a book in which the illustrations must play a primary role, both author and publisher wish to express their thanks to all those, photographers and librarians, who have given their co-operation, and first of all to Michel Regnault de la Mothe and Carlo Naccari for they help and advice.

Ancient Rome. The Palatine Hill from the Roman Forum. Opposite page, top, an illustration from «Hypnerotomachia Poliphili», Venice 1499; below, Piranesi, frontispiece from Volume 2 of «Antichità di Roma», Rome 1756.

The city of Rome is extremely difficult to describe and analyse both from a town-planning and an architectural point of view: in point of fact, it is not one, but four cities built one on top of another — cities that all played leading parts in the history of Europe — a palimpsest that was formed over a period of twenty-seven centuries. The ancient city which is still cleary defined by the enceinte of the Aurelian Walls (12 centuries), the medieval city (10 centuries) of which important remains still exist, particularly the splendid early-Christian and early Romanesque churches, then the Renaissance and Baroque city (four centuries) which was under direct papal government; finally the modern city (one century) built after 1871 when Rome became the capital of Italy. These four cities are, in a sense, hostile to each other: each one seems determined to suffocate the previous one, to hide it, even to eliminate it, yet all four of these cities are integral parts of Rome, even if we do sometimes have to search for them (with the exception of modern Rome which is unfortunately all too evident with its pompous Umbertine and post-Umbertine styles). No other city in the world boasts such a long and complex history. This brief synthesis of the development of the urban organism of Rome dealing mainly with the historic centre, enclosed within the ancient walls, is an introduction to the 101 sections which illustrate, albeit briefly, the history of the architecture of Rome from antiquity up to the present day.

The ancient city. According to tradition, Rome was founded in 753 B.C.: in fact traces of houses dating from the eighth century B.C. have been found on the Palatine; this is the period of the iron age, and one which saw the first Greek colonies in southern Italy (Ischia, Cuma). Around this original settlement which subsequently had its own defence system, the city gradually spread over the hills by the bend of the Tiber where the river, beyond the Tiber Island, could be easily forded. The city, inhabited by shepherds and peasants of various tribes — Latin, Sabine, Etruscan — developed thanks to its position on the route between Etruria, Latium and Campania. After the legendary period of the «Seven Kings», corresponding to the Etruscan domination, the Republic was founded (509 B.C.), and the city's importance increased steadily and its political and social organisation developed. Its centre was the Forum (no.4) which had been drained and paved by the seventh century. The earliest important temples were being built, the one on the Campidoglio, the acropolis of the city, dedicated to Jove Optimus Maximus, and those in the forum dedicated to Saturn and the Dioscuri. After the sack of Rome by the Gauls in 390 B.C., a mighty system of city walls, known as Servian or Republican, was constructed, enclosing the seven tradiitional hills (Palatine, Capitoline, Quirinal, Viminal, Esquiline, Celio and Aventine), and reaching the Tiber near the Forum Boarium (no. 10), the port area. In the third century, when Rome em-

The urban environment. Diagram of the hills of Rome showing the enceinte of the city walls of the Republican era; below, the area round the Baths of Caracalla in an engraving by Tempesta, 1593.

barked on her territorial expansion (conquering southern Italy, fighting the first Punic war, etc.) the city's inhabitants already numbered 100,000 The lie of the land obliged the city streets to be short and narrow, following the low-lying areas while the higher ground was occupied by the villas of the wealthiest landowners. This plan was largely maintained in the Imperial period so that the capital of the empire does not possess the characteristics of the planned cities based on an orthogonal street plan (castro and decumano). This lack of a geometrical town plan was not only due to the nature of the terrain but also to the laws governing land owning, typical of the Romans, which gave absolute supremacy to the rights of private property, making it «impossible for the state to expropriate land for reasons of public utility: sites for public buildings had to be bought on the free market. Caesar had to spend 100 million sestertii for the site needed to enlarge the Forum (Caesar's Forum)! (Quaroni).

The first attempt, only partly successful, to give the city what we would call a town plan was made by Julius Caesar himself, first with the Lex Julia Municipalis (45 B.C.) which set out ordinances concerning street maintenance and cleaning, traffic, aqueducts, sewers, police and fire services, etc. The Lex Julia de Modo Aedificiorum limited the height of buildings, particularly the «insulae», the large houses for renting which could not be higher than 20.8 metres (i.e. six or seven storeys); this gives us an idea of the population density in a city of about 800,000 inhabitants at the beginning of the Imperial era. In 45 B.C. Caesar passed a law regarding the growth of the city, Lex de Urbe Augenda; it regulated the area from Campus Martius north of the Campidoglio, beyond the Servian walls between via Flaminia and the bend of the Tiber — land which had already been settled. The river was to have been diverted from Ponte Milvio, returning to its bed near the Aventino, after flowing west of the Vatican and the Gianicolo. Caesar died the following year, and this ambitious plan was never carried out. Augustus later took up Caesar's idea, but without a definite plan, merely enlarging the administrative system to cover the **suburbio**, dividing the city into 14 districts, five of which were outside the walls. Augustus improved some public services: old aqueducts were repaired and new ones built, Aqua Vergine and Giulia, and commissioned some important monuments; the Forum of Augustus (no. 5) inside the walls, and the Baths of Agrippa in the Campus Martius area, (the first public baths), the Ara Pacis (no. 9), his own Mausoleum (no. 16), the Portico of Ottavia, the Pantheon (no. 12) and the large sundial with the Heliopolis obelisk now in front of Montecitorio (no. 70); it was said that Augustus had received a city of bricks and left one of stone behind him. The burning of Rome under Nero, whether or not it was caused by the Emperor himself, provided an important opportunity for a more rational reconstruction of the city. Nero took advantage of this to build himself a new palace, the famous Domus Aurea (no. 7), almost oriental in its splendour. His successors, Vespasian, Titus and

Domitian built many magnificent monuments on the site of Nero's palace which was largely destroyed: the Colosseum (no. 19), the Baths of Titus, and on the Palatine the enormous palace of the Emperor (no. 6). Another important urban development was Trajan's Forum and Markets, for which the Emperor demolished the hill linking the Campidoglio to the Quirinal (Trajan's column gives us an idea of its height), thus connecting the ancient city with Campus Martius. Under Hadrian, Roman architecture reached new heights with the construction of the Pantheon (no. 12) and Hadrian's Mausoleum, later known as Castel S. Angelo (no. 14). The city's new appearance was illustrated in an important document, the Forma Urbis, engraved on marble slabs in the early third century (no. 5). Sixty years later Aurelian built new walls to protect «a city, the like of which has never been seen on the face of the earth, marking its boundaries clearly, but, at the same time, limiting its future development», (Staccioli).

Diocletian and Maxentius, with their spectacular architecture, brought the history of ancient architecture to a close: their buildings are still today some of the most striking monuments in Rome, the Baths of Diocletian (no. 21) and the Basilica of Maxentius (no. 4). The history of Christian architecture begins with Constantine who built the last Baths on the Quirinal.

Despite all the destruction inflicted on Rome over the centuries, the ancient monuments can still give us an idea of what living in ancient Rome was like; «The basilicas and baths are the best examples of «opera aperta» in the history of architecture. They were constructions of great artistic interest for the use of all the citizens to meet together for all kinds of reasons, formal or informal, electoral meetings, business appointments, mere gossiping, public poetry recitals, relaxation, celebrations or important events. There was a sense of an area used by the people all day long and a feeling of architecture to be enjoyed as an urban facility, as a part of the city and as a work of art» (Quaroni).

The early-Christian and medieval city. Even before the fall of the Western Empire (476 A.D.) Rome was no longer an Imperial capital: the last Emperors preferred to reside elsewhere — Split, Milan, Ravenna or Constantinople. After the fall, the city, officially a Byzantine province, was conquered and sacked by the Goths and later by the Lombards; it was only after the rise of the Carolingian empire that it began at last to look like a capital city once again, where the emperors of the West were crowned. The temporal power of the popes which was making itself felt at this period was opposed in Rome itself both by the local aristocracy and, after 1143, by the municipality which from the Campidoglio tried unsuccessfully to impose its own power. Rome, once the centre of the most powerful empire in the world, had difficulty in governing itself. The papacy itself had religious difficulties to overcome such as the setbacks to the nomination of the anti-popes caused by the separation between the Greek Orthodox church and the Roman Catholics (1034).

The most problematical period in the whole history of Rome was when the papal see was transferred to Avignon (1309-77). When the Pope returned from exile in France, Rome probably had no more than 17,000 inhabitants: the population within the city walls had disappeared, leaving an empty ghost town consisting of ruins. The city had regressed to being the small community of shepherds it had once been. However, Rome continued to act as the religious centre of Catholic Europe during ten long centuries, albeit with some interruptions. As regards popular devotion, Rome was a place of pilgrimage as it contained the tomb of the apostle St. Peter. St. Peter's basilica was one of the wonders of the world, the largest church in Europe, a forest of columns lit by eighteen thousand lamps. This holy place, part of the «borgo» as it was outside the walls, was enclosed within its own defence system of fortified walls by Leo IVth (847-55), the «città Leonina».

During the first centuries of the Christian era, from the reign of Constantine onwards, prototypes of Christian architecture were developed in Rome: churches either had a basilica plan or a central plan (martyrium); Christian iconography representing religious stories, either frescoes, mosaics or sculpture, evolved from classical models which formed the basis of the Latin artistic tradition, as opposed to the oriental or byzantine style. After the Edict of Tolerance (313 A.D.), Constantine had already decided on the two Christian centres in Rome, the Lateran cathedral (no. 63), the bishop's see near the south east entrance to the city, and the basilica of St. Peter's (nos. 56 and 67) where the apostle had been buried, on the opposite side of the town (across the river, on the Vatican hill); thus Rome was two-headed. There are numerous churches inside the walls dating from the fourth and fifth centuries, built on sites where the early Christian martyrs lived or were killed or buried. By the early fifth century, Rome already had 25 parishes or «tituli»: churches such as S. Costanza (no. 22), S. Stefano Rotondo (no. 24), S. Sabina (no. 26), S. Agnese (no. 27), S. Maria in Cosmedin (no. 29), S. Maria in Domnica (no. 28) and S. Prassede (no. 30), are some of the purest examples of the whole Christian tradition, while the most important religious building inside the walls was that dedicated to the Virgin, S. Maria Maggiore (no. 25). The few inhabitants of Rome in this period lived in the area Campus Martius, between the Campidoglio and the S. Angelo bridge; the Campidoglio had traditionally been the administrative centre of the city, and during the third century the Senatorial Palace had been built there to house the municipal offices. Nearby the fortified residences of the rich feudal families were built — the Annibaldis, the Colonnas, the Contis, the Caetanis, etc.: their towers are the most important examples of civil buildings in medieval Rome. Around this nucleus which occupied only a small part of the area inside the ancient walls, Renaissance and Baroque Rome

Popes of the Renaissance. From top to bottom: (1) detail from «Handing over the keys» by Perugino, 1481, Sistine Chapel, fresco commissioned by Sixtus IV Della Rovere (c.f.p. 72); (2) Michelangelo, Moses on the tomb of Julius II Della Rovere (1513-16) in the church of S. Pietro in Vincoli; (3) Titian, Portrait of Paul III Farnese with his nephews (detail), 1546, Capodimonte Museum, Naples.

was to develop later on — the heart of the papal capital as it was up to the end of the last century

The Renaissance city. The history of Renaissance Rome, the modern city, could be said to begin with the definitive transfer of the papal residence from the Lateran Palace to the Vatican under Nicholas V (1447-55). In the space of a little more than two centuries — the 16th and the 17th — Rome took on the Classical-Baroque aspect which we still recognise today. Not only did Nicholas V decide to remove the papal see to the Vatican, defended by medieval walls as well as by the great mass of Hadrian's Mausoleum, which had been transformed into a fortress, but he also considered rebuilding the thousand-year old basilica of Constantine — a project which was carried out at the beginning of the following century. In 1464 the Venetian Pietro Barbo was elected Pope, Paolo II: he chose Palazzo Venezia as his official residence (no. 40), a building he had begun in 1445 when he was the cardinal of the nearby church of S. Marco. This decision indicated a new policy on the part of the church towards the city: the intention was to make the whole of Rome a papal city — the new residence is right in the middle of the capital, close to the Campidoglio from which Rome was governed. «The substance of the Paoline Statutes proposed the formal conservation of local administrative autonomy, but aimed at identifying municipal finances with the treasure of St. Peter's. Paolo II was convinced that the papacy could not be Roman unless Rome was under the jurisdiction of the Pope. Paolo was an able diplomat thanks to his Venetian origins, and a master of compromise» (Insolera). Palazzo Venezia was to remain the papal residence for a whole century, until the mid-sixteenth century when the Pope transferred his residence to the nearby Quirinal (no. 62).

The papacy showed more interest in rebuilding the city towards the end of the fifteenth century, particularly with Sixtus IV della Rovere (1471-84), described as the restorer of the city; he restored religious and secular buildings such as S. Maria del Popolo (no. 43), the Sistine Chapel, the Vatican Library and the Hospital of the Santo Spirito. Important urban structures were also planned: the Ponte Sisto (no. 42), the restoration of the Vergine aqueduct, the construction of the road system leading to Ponte S. Angelo (Via Paola, Via Banco di S. Spirito, Via di Panico); the construction of districts for Dalmatians or 'Schiavoni', refugees from the Turkish invasion (Hospital and Church of S. Girolamo) and for the Lombards (Hospital and Church of S. Ambrogio), in the area between the Mausoleum of Augustus and Porto di Ripetta; the local market was moved from the Campidoglio to Piazza Navona.

Alexander VI Borgia (1492-1503) and Giulio II della Rovere (1503-13) concentrated their attention in a most decisive way on the Vatican itself. Alexander rebuilt the Borgo Nuovo, making it into an aristocratic residential area, then Giulio summoned the most famous artists and architects of the period, Bramante, Raffaello, Michelangelo and many others to Rome to make the Vatican into the most magnificent court of Europe at that time: St. Peter's was rebuilt, (no. 56), new palaces in the Vatican were built and decorated (no. 46).

Giulio II also made new streets leading from the Vatican, the Via Giulia on the left bank of the Tiber, and on the opposite bank, Via della Lungara; meanwhile Via dei Banchi (now Via del Banco di Santo Spirito) had become an international financial centre where Italian and foreign bankers such as the Chigi and Fugger families had their offices. The fifty years from 1515-1565 were the most important for the construction of the Renaissance city under the enterprising Popes who included Leo X Medici (1513-21), Clement VII Medici (1523-34), Paolo III Farnese (1534-49), Giulio III Ciocchi (1550-55), Paolo IV Carafa (1555-59) and Pius IV Medici (1559-65). The enormous cost of rebuilding S. Pietro was one of the main causes of the Lutheran protest (1517), one of the most far-reaching religious movements in modern history (the costs of S. Pietro were met partly by the sale of indulgences); the Roman Catholic Counter-Reformation followed soon afterwards (the Council of Trent ended in 1563). Apparently neither this dramatic religious schism, nor the Sack of Rome by the Imperial troops in 1527 had any effect on the great artistic and building projects carried out by popes and cardinals in this period. During these extraordinary fifty years Michelangelo's work on S. Pietro (no. 56), the Campidoglio and the frescoes in the Sistine Chapel were carried out, as well as the construction of Palazzo Vidoni Cattarelli (no. 49), Villa Madama (no. 48), Palazzo Farnese (no. 53), Palazzo Massimo alle Colonne (no. 52), Villa Giulia (no. 58) etc. — some of the most influential buildings in the history of European architecture. In the field of town-planning, many new roads were being built: the three roads, «tridente», leading off Piazza del Popolo, Via Leonina (now Via di Ripetta), and Via Paolina Trifaria (now Via del Babuino); also Via Trinità (now Via Condotti, Via di Fontanella Borghese and via del Clementino) which linked Piazza di Spagna, the embassy area, with Porto Ripetta. Via Pia (via XX Settembre) was conceived by Pius IV: it crossed the Quirinal area where there were many important villas of cardinals, thus becoming an aristocratic street leading to Porta Pia, where Michelangelo had built the church of S. Maria degli Angeli (no. 21).

In 1526 the first census of the population of Rome was carried out: the city had 55,000 inhabitants, mostly concentrated within the bend of the Tiber, near Ponte S. Angelo; the rest of the city was more or less open countryside — wide stretches of vineyards and gardens in the midst of which stood isolated abandoned ruins of ancient Rome. The most important of these monuments had been intact up to the fifteenth century: their destruction was due neither to barbarians nor to the passing of time, but to the planned demolition by the Renaissance builders. From the mid-fifteenth century onwards, these ruins were used as a source of building materials for the new

constructions under way. Raffaello, who can be considered the father of modern archeology, wrote to Leo X: «How many popes have allowed the destruction of ancient temples, statues, arches and other buildings, the glory of ancient Rome? How much cement has been made of ancient statues and other ornaments? It is with regret that I observe that although I have only been living in Rome for twelve years, many beautiful objects have been destroyed during that time...».

The archeologist, Rodolfo Lanciani, made the first survey of the ancient city in the late 19th century, observing that «the great masters of the Renaissance treated our monuments and ruins with incredible contempt and brutality». He recalled that an official document, discovered by Eugenio Müntz in the State Archives of Rome, certified that in the year 1452, one of the city contractors called Giovanni Foglia from Como, carried away 2522 cartloads of travertine.

The last decades of the sixteenth century saw a great change in the religious and cultural climate of Rome; with Pius V Ghisleri (1566-72), Gregorio XIII Boncompagni (1572-85), and particularly with Sixtus V Peretti (1585-90), the Counter-Reformation began in earnest. At this time religious orders began to commission buildings, the most influential of these were the Jesuits for whom Vignola built the mother church, Gesù (no. 61). The city plan continued to be developed; Gregory XIII built the Quirinal Palace (no. 62) and laid out Piazzale di Termini (the name comes from the nearby **terme** or baths), continuing the work of Pius IV (via Pia, S. Maria degli Angeli), and transformed one «rotonda» of the baths into the church of S. Bernardo (no. 65). The square became the main centre for the distribution of agricultural produce (with warehouses for grain, oil, etc.). Sixtus V completed the Termini with the construction of the Fontana Felice (no. 101). The buildings were simpler, in harmony with the new austerity, and Domenico Fontana, counsellor to Sixtus V, was the architect who best interpreted this spirit; he designed the two buildings which were characteristic of the Counter-Reformation, the Vatican Palace overlooking Piazza S. Pietro and that of the Lateran (no. 63): palaces that were «conceived as rigid blocks, strictly adhering to the two orthogonal axes of symmetry, austere volumes which could be inserted into any townscape». (Insolera).

Sixtus V saw Rome as the triumphant capital of the new catholicism of the Counter-Reformation, a place of pilgrimage first of all, as well as the seat of the head of the church. With the Sistine plan, Rome became the first city in Europe with a road system linking all the main religious buildings. This plan is illustrated in two contemporary maps of the city, that of the Seven Churches by Antonio Lafrery (1575), and the street plan included in the biography of Sixtus V by Bordsino (1588). Lafrery's map shows the seven basilicas that the pilgrim must visit in Rome: S. Pietro, S. Maria Maggiore, S. Giovanni in Laterano, S. Croce in Gerusalemme, S. Paolo fuori le Mura, S. Sebastiano and S. Lorenzo. The map, in the medieval tradition, is purely symbolic, the topog-

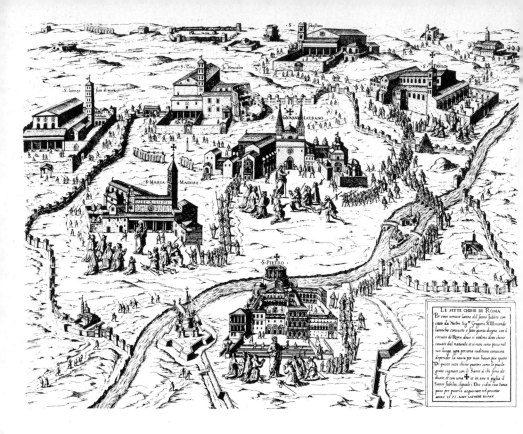

raphy schematic, but the churches are carefully drawn, giving us an idea of what these buildings were like in their original Early-Christian form; only S. Pietro shows the tambour of the cupola which Michelangelo had not managed to complete. Sixtus V commissioned Domenico Fontana to draw up this plan linking old and new roads in a single street system; at focal points in front of the main churches he set up some of the obelisks which were to become symbols of the city, particularly the one in front of S. Pietro. The town plan goes from Porta Flaminia and S. Pietro and has the basilica of S. Maria Maggiore (no. 25) in the centre with roads spreading out in all directions from it, like a star; in fact devotion to the Virgin Mary was one of the main tenets of the Counter-Reformation, in contrast to the Protestant Reformation which had abolished the veneration of Mary.

This basilica, the earliest and most important dedicated to the Virgin, had already been embellished by Michelangelo's Sforza chapel, and was subsequently enlarged by the construction of the Cappella Sistina, built as Sixtus' burial place, and the Cappella Paolina built by Paolo V. The roads made by Sixtus are the via Felice (now via Sistina, via Quattro Fontane and via de Petris), beyond the basilica the road continued as far as S. Croce in Gerusalemme, making a straight stretch of 3,300 metres; via Panisperna leading from Piazza Venezia to S. Maria Maggiore; via S. Giovanni in Laterano leading from the basilica to the Colosseum. The link between S. Giovanni in Laterano and S. Paolo fuori le Mura was not carried out, and the via Merulana leading from S. Maria Maggiore to the basilica of S. Giovanni had already been laid out by Gregory XIII. Modern Rome was thus defined for the next three centuries, contained within two triangles on a common base with vertices at Porta del Popolo and the Campidoglio.

The Baroque city. Paul V Borghese (1605-21) completed this project of Sixtus', dedicated to the Virgin, by building a new patriarchal palace near the basilica of S. Maria Maggiore, and his chapel inside the church as mentioned above; he then laid out via Paolina in line with the chapel and placed a column in front of the basilica. He carried out a similar plan in Trastevere involving another church dedicated to the Virgin, S. Maria in Trastevere; provided the water supply to the district with the Acquedotto Paolo and the Fontana Paola as Sixtus V had done with the Termini quarter.

The period of Roman Baroque really began under Pope Urban VIII Barberini (1623-44) with artists and architects of the stature of Bernini,

Borromini and Pietro da Cortona. He first completed his family palace in via delle Quattro Fontane (no. 66), then commissioned Bernini to design the great baldacchino in S. Pietro. Under this papacy the outer defence walls were strengthened by the construction of walls round Trastevere which join onto those of the Vatican. The Baroque period reached its peak under Alexander VII Chigi (1655-67), as regards development of the city with Piazza S. Pietro (no. 67), Piazza S. Maria della Pace (no. 73) and Piazza del Popolo (no. 82). At this time Rome had a population of 125,000 inhabitants.

However, much of Baroque Rome was not built by the popes alone: many of its finest monuments were created by various members of the great papal families. The figure of the cardinal-nephew is characteristic of seventeeth and eighteenth-century Rome: «The cardinal-nephew is at the same time the secretary and confidant of the pope-uncle, his private agent, his manager; he has a humanistic education and is an expert on doctrine, he prefers the figurative arts to literature, but towards the eighteenth century, patronised music and the theatre as well. He is a great collector of archeological remains, as well as being organiser, financer and promoter of excavations» (Insolera). Villa Borghese (no. 64) is undoubtedly the best preserved example of this artistic patronage, with its extraordinary collection of antique and modern masterpieces. These building were generally villas with extensive grounds, such as Villa Ludovisi which had «the most beautiful garden in the world» (unfortunately destroyed in the late nineteenth century). The name of the Pamphili family is connected with Piazza Navona (no. 79), where the family had its palace, with Via del Corso (no. 87), as well as with Villa Doria Pamphili on the Aurelia, which still has its large park intact, designed by Alessadro Algardi in 1644.

This tradition of the cardinals' villas forming a green belt all round the historic centre continued during the eighteenth century, even though the Papal State was no longer the political and economic power it had been during the two previous centuries. Rome was still one of the great artistic capitals of Europe, and one of the most famous artistic centres of the eighteenth century was a Roman villa, that of cardinal Albani (no. 90), where meetings took place between Winckelmann and Mengs, the great theorists of neo-classicism. During the mid-eighteenth century two important engravers were working in Rome, both connected in some way with Albani, who have left us a unique documentation of the city — Giovanni Battista Nolli and Giovanni Battista Piranesi.

Nolli (1692-1756), born in Como, came to Rome about 1736 and set to work to make a complete plan of the whole city of Rome which was published in 1748 after 12 years' work; it was the most perfect scientific representation of a city which had yet been carried out. Nolli, this pioneer of the technique of map-making, described every detail of the city, both the built-up parts and the open countryside outside the walls with its gar-

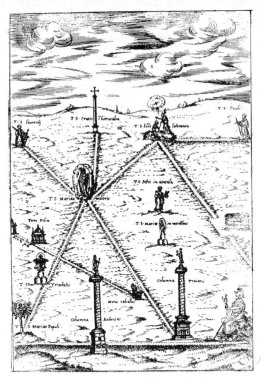

Sixtus V's plan. Above, Diagram of the Sistine roads in the biography of Sixtus V Peretti by Bordino (1588); opposite page, «The seven churches of Rome», engraving by Lafréry, 1575; below, this page, plan of the roads built between 1450 (Nicholas V) and 1621 (Paul V), those indicated by dotted lines were not carried out.

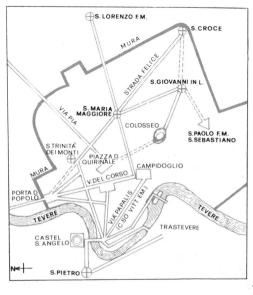

dens and orchards; it was to remain like this up to the end of the nineteenth century.

This green belt is classified by Nolli into three categories — villas, vineyards and kitchen gardens. In his analysis of the map, Insolera mentions 127 villas, 246 vineyards and 68 kitchen gardens: inside the walls there are 99, 119 and 38 of these three classifications. The romantic ideal of the countryside inside the city, the most original contribution made by eighteenth-century English civilisation, already existed in Rome, therefore, — a city which the inventors of landscape gardening, Lord Burlington and William Kent, knew well. Piranesi (1720-78) was part of the retinue of the Venetian ambassador Francesco Venier who was appointed to represent Venice in the papal State in 1740. After this first visit to Rome, four years later he returned, this time for good, working as an engraver. He had been trained as an architect — all his family were builders: his uncle Matteo Lucchesi was part of that team of technical experts and hydraulic engineers working with the Magistrato alle Acque, together with Tiralli and Temanza. Piranesi began his career in Rome working with Nolli on the map of the Tiber (1744) and that of the city. In his engravings of «Antichità Romane» (1756) and especially in those of the Castello dell'Acqua Claudia (1761) and of the water flowing out of Lake Albano (1762) we can see that he was a competent engineer, including details as though he was illustrating Diderot's Encyclopedia. As Focillon wrote, Piranesi can be considered the founder of modern archeology. Despite their precision, Piranesi's views are carried out in an extremely free style — a technique he learned from Tiepolo — giving us an almost visionary representation of what Rome must have been at the time of its greatest splendour. His imaginative reconstruction of Campus Martius (1762) was to inspire the architects contemporary with the French Revolution in their plans for the ideal city (Boullée, Ledoux, Soane).

The Rome of Nolli and Piranesi, before the destruction carried out in the late nineteenth and early twentieth centuries, might be described as the perfect city, within the limits of historical reality. During the first half of the 18th century, many urban improvements were carried out: perhaps this was the best period of Roman town planning when architects worked to the benefit of the city in a functional and civilised way. The port of Ripetta, the Trevi Fountain (no. 101), Piazza S. Ignazio (no. 85), the steps of Trinità dei Monti (no. 84) are all masterpieces of the late Baroque period, while Piazza del Popolo (no. 92), the most important piece of urban planning in the neo-classical period, crowns the classical-Baroque aspect of the city, after three centuries.

The modern city. On July 31st 1871, Rome became the capital of the new kingdom of Italy; its 200,000 inhabitants doubled in twenty years, becoming almost a million by the 1930s. Up to the sixteenth century, even the largest European cities had few more than 150,000 inhabitants; it was only from the seventeenth century onwards that city populations increased dramatically. At the start of that century London and Paris had about 200,000, inhabitants each — not many more than Rome. By the end of the century, however, London had reached 800,000 and Paris 700,000; a century later, after the Industrial Revolution, these cities had swollen each to become a vast metropolis. By the beginning of the present century London had over four million inhabitants and Paris about two million. The growth of Rome was far more sudden than that of London and Paris: it took place over a brief period of a few decades in the historic centre, within the walls. It should be noted that the historic centre of Rome was both larger and more important than those of other European cities, including London and Paris, and thus new buildings should have been planned with great caution. All the town-planning experts of the period, such as Stubben and Haussmann (who had a completely free hand in replanning Paris), suggested building the new city outside the walls, in order to preserve the monumental quality of the centre and the green formed by the great villas and their grounds. However, it was decided otherwise.

Land values increased enormously during the first few years of Italian administration, giving rise to aggressive building speculation: prices increased from tenfold, and in the most central areas, a hundredfold. The 1873 city plan provided for concentrated building inside and immediately outside the city walls: the Ludovisi district near Porta Pinciana which involved the destruction of a large garden, scandalising the whole of Europe; the area Piazza Indipendenza, east of the Termini station; that near S. Maria Maggiore in the Esquilino district, and further south, the district round the Colosseum and at Testaccio. Beyond the Tiber much new building was carried out in Trastevere and to the north of the Vatican in the Prati district. This plan permitted many 'improvements' i.e. works of demolition right in the centre, such as Corso Vittorio Emanuele (the most ruinous). In the thirties, during the Fascist period, the most disastrous transformation schemes were those of Via dei Fori Imperiali and Via della Conciliazione leading to S. Pietro, where Bernini himself wanted a screen (a third row of columns) so as to emphasise the sudden opening out of the square after passing through winding narrow streets. During the past 40 years, the city has continued to spread with no real town plan; there are occasional exceptions of some merit such as the Tiburtino district and EUR. In one century Rome's population increased from 200,000 to 3,000,000, a monstrous increase of fifteenfold! It is something of a miracle that the city continues to function at all, and that there is still a human dimension around at least some of the finest buildings in our history. In conclusion, one of the few culturally valid undertakings carried out at the beginning of the century should be mentioned, the plan of the archeological sites of the city drawn up by Rodolfo Lanciani, the «Forma Urbis Romae» on a 1:1000 scale (1901); this maps out with great precision the remains and sites of ancient buildings, a valuable document which gives us some idea of what the city was like in past centuries.

Despite the happenings of the past hundred years, Rome remains an extraordinarily fascinating city, one that affords us aesthetic and intellectual experiences that are highly stimulating (it is in Rome that we discover at every corner the prototypes of so much Italian and European architecture); it also offers us a particularly pleasing environment as regards air, light, colours, stones, marble, stucco, walls, courtyards, the lie of the land, abundant water, food — the bread, wine, cheeses and vegetables are generally excellent. We feel that the countryside, nature, is not far away, that the real city which has grown up on this ancient site, the old organism that is Rome, is not a museum, does not live in the past alone, but is alive and still capable of surprising the world as it has done in the past.

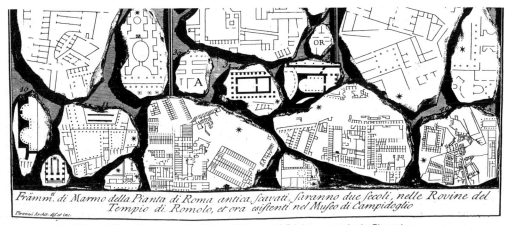

Frammᵗⁱ di Marmo della Pianta di Roma antica ſcavati ſaranno due ſecoli, nelle Rovine del Tempio di Romolo, et ora esiſtenti nel Muſeo di Campidoglio

Piranesi Archit: delſ et inc.

Fragments of the «Forma Urbis», the ancient plan of Rome (3rd century A.D.), in an engraving by Piranesi.

Bibliography

«Immagine di Roma» by *Ludovico Quaroni* (Laterza, Bari, 1976) and «Roma» by Italo Insolera (Laterza, Bari, 1985), both in the series «Le Città nella d'Italia», are written by specialists but can be enjoyed by the general reader: they are complementary and together form an introduction to the complex history of the urban development of Rome; Insolera's book has excellent illustrations, and both volumes have a complete bibliography. *Nikolaus Pevsner's* «An Outline ofEuropean Architecture», (Pelican Books, Harmondsworth, 1943) and *Sir Banister Fletcher's* «A History of Architecture» (19th edition, edited by John Musgrove, Butterworth Architecture, 1987) are indispensable for the understanding of the history of architecture. Equally important for the art and architecture of ancient Rome are *Bianchi Bandinelli's* studies «Roma: L'arte Romana nel centro del Potere», and «Roma. La fine dell'arte antica», both in the series «Il mondo della figura», Rizzoli, Milan, 1979. The archeological itineraries of *Romolo Straccioli*, «Roma entro le mura», and *Stefania Quilici Gigli*, «Roma fuori le mura», (both published by Newton Compton, Milan, 1979 and 1980 respectively), are exemplary. *Richard Krautheimer*, one of the greatest experts on the middle ages, is the author of «Rome, Profile of a city, 312-1308» (Princeton University Press, 1980) and of «Three Christian Capitals: Rome, Milan and Constantinople: Topography and Politics» (University of California Press, Berkeley, 1983).

Of the many books on the Renaissance period, the following should be mentioned: *Leonardo Benevolo* «Storia dell'architettura del Rinascimento» (Laterza, Bari, 1978); *Peter Murray* «The Architecture of the Italian Renaissance» (Thames and Hudson, London, 1969); *André Chastel* «Les Grands Ateliers d'Italie» (Gallimard, Paris, 1965); *Heydenreich and Passavant* «Le temps des Génies dans la Renaissance Italienne; 1500-1540» (Gallimard, Paris, 1974). These studies deal with all forms of artistic expression over the whole of Italy, but the monuments of Rome form an important sector. Books on the Baroque period are equally numerous; the 17th and 18th centuries when much of the Rome we know today was built. *Rudolf Wittkower's* «Art and Architecture in Italy, 1600-1750» (Pelican Books, Harmondsworth, 1958) is indispensable. *Paolo Portoghesi's* «Roma Barocca» (Laterza, Bari, 1973) deals specifically with the architecture of the period. *Anthony Blunt's* «Guide to Baroque Rome» is both sympathetic yet complete (Granada, London, 1982). The study of *Cassanelli, Delfini and Fonti* «Le Mura di Roma» (Bulzoni, Roma, 1974) emphasises the importance of military architecture in the city and traces its development from ancient Rome up to modern times from an original point of view.

As regards modern architecture, *Manfredo Tafuri's* «Storia dell'architettura Italiana 1944-85» (Einaudi, Turin, 1982) is one of the most up-to-date studies and, for a wider survey, «Modern Architecture in Europe» by *D.J. and E.R. De Witt* (Weidenfeld and Nicolson, London, 1987). «Lo Stato pontificio da Martino IV a Pio IX» by *Mario Caravale* and *Alberto Caracciolo* in the Utet series «Storia d'Italia» (1986) is a good political history of the papal city from the return from Avignon up to the unification of Italy.

As regards guide books, «Roma e dintorni» of the *Touring Club Italiano* (1977) is a standard work, whereas Georgina Masson's «The Companion Guide to Rome» (Fontana, Collins, 1955) makes delightful reading, brimming with all kinds of information. A good guide to the architecture is *Sylvia Pressouyre's* «Rome au fil du temps», (Cuenot, Paris, 1973). Finally a classical book on Rome is «Edifices de Rome Moderne» by *Paul Letarouilly* (facsimile of 1840 original, Butterworth Architecture, 1982).

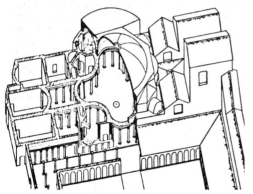

Hadrian's Villa at Tivoli. Top, the nympheum and the canal of Canopo; above left, reconstruction of the domed hall of the Piazza d'Oro (from Quilici Gigli's «Roma fuori le Mura»).

Ostia. Left, Residential houses; above right, Reconstruction of the courtyard of Diana's house, according to Gismondi.

ANCIENT ARCHITECTURE

The ancient Romans were practical people whose main interest was the spreading and consolidation of their dominion over ever-growing regions; they showed scant interest in the visual arts, sculptors and painters were almost all artists of Greek origin. They were interested in architecture connected with war (roads, bridges, fortifications) and in building public edifices for the purposes of the administration or the glorification of the State. Although architectural forms and canons were always of Greek origin (e.g. architectural orders), the use made of them was completely original. Whereas Greek architecture is based on vertical and horizontal lines (columns and trabeation), a sort of «sublime carpentry» as it has been described, with the prevailing use of stone as building material, Roman architecture is plastic, based on the curved line (arch, vault, cupola, etc.) with wide use of cement and brickwork, humble materials which were faced with stone, marble, stucco and frescoes. The first important use of the arch and vault is to be found in the Tabularium, 79 B.C. (no. 4); important utility constructions typical of the Romans such as aqueducts and early bridges, date from the fourth century B.C. (no. 3). The great period of Roman architecture began with Caesar and Augustus; Caesar built the first forum on a regular plan which was to be followed by a series of piazzas to celebrate various emperors (no. 5). The Augustan era imposed the classical tradition (it might even be called neo-classical) both in architecture and sculpture (Forum and Mausoleum of Augustus, the Ara Pacis and the theatre of Marcellus all in Rome; abroad, especially in Gallia, the Maison Carrée in Nîmes, the theatre in Orange, etc.). Under Nero (54-68) famous for the Domus Aurea, Greek and oriental influences predominate. Under the Flavi, with Titus (79-81) the Arch of Titus and the Colosseum; under Domitian (81-96) the new Imperial Palace on the Palatine; under Trajan (98-117) the great Forum with the nearby markets and new baths, and lastly under Hadrian (117-138), the Pantheon, the Mausoleum and the Villa at Tivoli, Roman architecture reaches its greatest glory. Under the Severi, Septimius Severus (193-211) with his new palace on the Palatine and Triumphal arch, and Caracalla (198-217), the buildings become increasingly grandiose and complex, culminating in the magnificence of the Aurelian Walls (270-75) and in the extraordinary monuments left by Diocletian (284-305), the baths and the enormous palace in Split, just when the empire was beginning to crumble. Maxentius (306-337) and Constantine can be considered the last great Roman builders, even though this period was drawing to a close and the barbaric Middle Ages were imminent. Rome boasts many ancient buildings, but no examples of dwelling houses remain, which must have formed the very fabric of the city. For examples of this kind of building we must go to Pompei, with its typical upper-class dwellings based on the peristyle, or those at Ostia, the port of Rome, where many-storeyed lower-class buildings (**insulae**) are well preserved, typical of economic housing in imperial Rome. Hadrian's villa at Tivoli near Rome, (c. 126 A.D.) exemplifies the type of aristocratic residence, frequent in the Roman countryside: here the building interprets «Roman Baroque», derived from late Hellenism, in a sumptuous way, as do the Temple of Minerva Medica (no. 17) and the great Baths of Caracalla (no. 20) and of Diocletian (no. 21).

Antique stucco work in an engraving by Piranesi.

Roman engineering. Roman architecture is in the first place «technical skill in the service of government of public affairs» (Argan), i.e. engineering based not on the marble block of the Greeks, but on **opus caementicium,** a mixture of mortar and gravel faced with brickwork: an extremely flexible method of construction as well as one that was extremely strong, suitable for the curved lines of the arch, the basic element of Roman structure which could become vault, cupola, apse, etc.; it enabled the Roman builders to construct works of enormous size and complexity. In fact, it is in the purely utilitarian constructions such as bridges, aqueducts, sewers, fortifications and roads that Roman building achieved its greatest results. The road is perhaps the most important achievement of Roman engineers — a means to dominate territories, but also to serve the people; roads implied bridges for crossing rivers, embankments over low-lying land, and tunnels under the mountains. Roadmaking was a complicated, laborious process which began with cutting a trench 4 metres wide, 1 or 2 metres deep, which was then filled in with several layers of sand, gravel and stones before the surface layer composed of large polygonal rocks fitted together with great precision. These highly functional works were technically perfect, and were carried out traditionally by the army legions; these, therefore were not merely forces for war, but also an efficient organisation of labour for public works; civil and military engineering were synonymous for the Romans. Von Hagen observes «Roman roads had an incalculable importance in the whole history of humanity. Rome became a mobile source of civilisation and master of the world largely because it succeeded in controlling a large part of the surface of the known world, thanks to its roads».

From top to bottom, (1) Detail of a building in Ostia; (2) Construction technique illustrated in an engraving by Piranesi (cement rubble filling the space between two brick walls); (3) **Roman roads**. Plan of the main Roman roads during the Imperial period.

Porta Appia or Porta S. Sebastiano.

View of the Aurelian Walls.

1

CITY WALLS AND GATES 4th century B.C. - 5th century A.D. The earliest city walls, known as «Servian» as they were traditionally ascribed to Servius Tullius (mid 6th century B.C.), are those built after the sack of Rome by the Gauls, i.e. from 378 B.C. onwards. They were nearly 11 kms long, encircling the seven traditional hills of Rome (about 426 hectares). These walls were built of blocks of tufa stone: they were 4-10 metres wide and up to 10 metres high. On the inside, where the land was flat, ramparts 30-40 metres wide were built against the walls, while on the outside a ditch 30 metres wide and 17 metres deep was dug. The best preserved remains we have are those near the **Termini** train station (no. 97), about 100 metres long. This mighty bulwark of the Republican city was not replaced for six and half centuries when the Aurelian Walls were built by the emperor Aurelian (270-275), when the presence of barbarians on the northeast borders threatened the empire. The Aurelian Walls are almost double the length of the original defences, enclosing the largest city in Europe, from the Pincio in the north to the Janiculum on the right bank of the Tiber. They were 6-8 metres high and 3.5 wide, with slits and square turrets every 30 metres; there were great gates (the most important had two arches) where the main roads entered the city: clockwise from the north, the Porta Flaminia or del Popolo, the Pinciana, the Salaria, the Nomentana, the Tiburtina or S. Lorenzo, the Prenestina or Porta Maggiore, the Asinara, the Metronia, the Latina, the Appia or S. Sebastiano, the Ostiense or S. Paolo, then towards Trastevere, the Portuense and the Aurelia were the most important. These gates were protected by a semicircular tower on either side, crowned by battlements. The Aurelian Walls were strengthened at the beginning of the 4th century by Maxentius by the addition of an external trench, and further reinforced and made higher by Honorius (401-2) when the threat of invasion by the Goths increased. This mighty bulwark remains largely intact and is «one of the most important and interesting monuments of Ancient Rome» (Staccioli). The best preserved city gate is the **Appia** (S. Sebastiano): it originally had two arches, what we see is Honorius' rebuilding. On the inside there is a fortified courtyard and the Arch of Drusus, actually an arch of Caracalla's aqueduct (Aqua Antonina) supplying water to his Baths; it now forms a monumental entrance to the Via Appia. On either side of the arch the grooves for lowering the portcullis from the upper storey can be seen (there is an interesting museum of the Walls inside the gate building). A long stretch of the walls runs west from this gate with various **square towers** up to the bastion (300 metres) built by Antonio da Sangallo the Younger in 1536. The **Ostiense gate** is also remarkable for its state of preservation, with its fortified courtyard; it houses the Via Ostiense Museum devoted to the port of Rome and the excavations at Ostia. Nearby, the walls surround

25

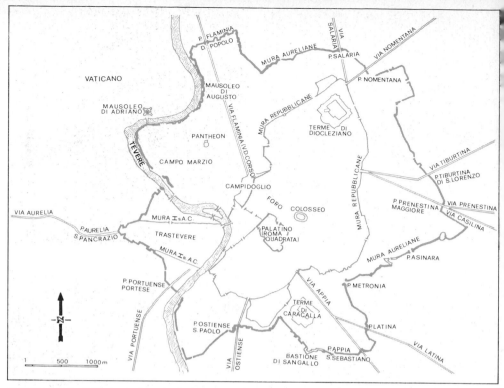

Plan of the Aurelian Walls showing the main city gates.

the adjoining **Cestius' pyramid** (no. 16), as a further bulwark. The walls start again on the far bank of the Tiber: on the banks were two medieval towers, since destroyed, and here the river could be blocked in emergencies by iron chains. Up river from Ponte Sisto, the walls continued along the left bank up to the Porta Flaminia which was completely rebuilt in the sixteenth century. Nearby stands the Muro Torto supporting the Acilii gardens above, dating from the late republican period and subsequently incorporated in the Aurelian Walls; this was a district of villas and gardens up to imperial times. The walls between the Porta Pinciana and the Salaria are well preserved. After the Porta Nomentana, the walls make a rectangular detour to include the Castro Pretorio, the barracks of the Praetorian Guard built by Tiberius (20-23 A.D.). Near Piazzale Sixtus V the arches of Aqua Marcia can be seen, built by Diocletian for his baths, an aqueduct that was restored by Pius V and Sixtus V for Aqua Felice. The Porta Tiburtina incorporates in its Augustan arch the Marcia, Tepula and Julia aqueducts. Next we have the impressive structure of the **Porta Prenestina (Maggiore)**, an archway for entering the city built by

the emperor Claudius as part of his aqueduct in 38-52 A.D. (no. 3) The next part of the walls include the arches of the same aqueduct by Claudius and nearby, the edge of the Anfiteatro Castrense. Before we end our tour of the walls at the Porta Appia, the **Porta Latina** is worth noting as it is one of the best preserved: the semicircular tower on the left is almost intact.

It was not until the 9th century that an important addition was made to the ancient defence system — the building of the Leonine City, when Leo IV (847-55) included in a single enceinte both the basilica of S. Pietro and Hadrian's Mausoleum (now Castel Sant'Angelo, no. 14). The next improvement was made by Nicolas V (1447-55), who transformed Castel Sant'Angelo into a real fortress, adding three corner towers. During the 16th century Paul III Farnese ordered **Antonio Sangallo the Younger** to build fortifications: the ardeatine Bastions (1537-46) which were never completed. **Michelangelo** was commissioned to build **Porta Pia** (1561-64) at the end of the newly-built Via Pia, a development of Pius IV's. Lastly, Urban VIII Barberini (1623-44) surrounded the Gianicolo with bastions, thus including it in the Vatican defence system.

Porta Ostiense or Porta S. Paolo.

Porta Prenestina or Porta Maggiore.

Porta Asinara.

Porta Latina.

Sangallo the Younger: Ardeatine bastions, 1537-46.

Michelangelo, Porta Pia, 1561-64.

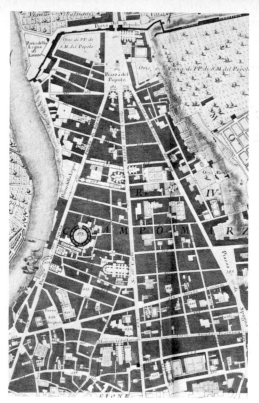

Via Flaminia. Via del Corso, formerly Via Flaminia, also known as Via Lata, as shown in Nolli's map, 1748.

Ancient road surfaces. Top, Detail of an engraving by Piranesi; below, the paving of Via Appia.

2

THE ROADS, 4th - 3rd century B.C. The Milliarum Aureum, the column placed in the Forum by Augustus, just below the Campidoglio, marked the ideal starting point of roads that led to the very end of the known world; their number increased over the centuries, and under Domitian they covered 80,000 kms. The earliest Roman road is the **Appia**, the **regina viarum**, begun in 312 B.C.; nearly as old are the Tiburtina (307 B.C.) going to Tivoli, the Aurelia (241 B.C.) leading north along the Tyrrhenian coast and the **Flaminia**, (220 B.C.) perhaps the most important from a strategic point of view. The Via Flaminia, which follows the modern **Via del Corso**, crossed the peninsula in a north-easterly direction, reaching the Adriatic Sea at Fano, continuing along the coast to Rimini, where the Via Emilia branched off to the north west towards Turin and France, while the Via Annia continued north from Rimini to Aquileia and Eastern Europe. The Via Claudia Augusta went from Altino on the lagoon of Venice to connect Rome with the Danube. The Via Flaminia was the spinal column of Roman territorial aggrandisement in the north of Italy and hence to the rest of Europe. However, the Via Appia is the best preserved and the most interesting, leading from the Porta Capena of the original Servian walls, just below the Palatine, on the route of the modern Via delle Terme and Via di Porta S. Sebastiano, towards the Alban hills to Capua. In 191 B.C. it was continued as far as Benevento and Brindisi; later, under the name of Via Appia Traiana it reached Bari on the southern Adriatic coast. The Via Appia went in the opposite direction to that of the Flaminia — to the south for trade with Greece, the Middle East and Africa. The 20 kilometres between the gates of Rome and the Alban hills form an archeological park; much of the paving remains, and on either side of the road there are traces of villas, temples and tombs including the Mausoleum of Cecilia Metella (no. 15), one of the most famous monuments of the late republican period.

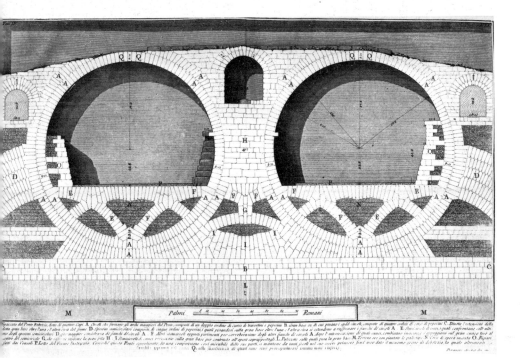

Section of Ponte Fabricio in an engraving by Piranesi.

3

BRIDGES AND AQUEDUCTS, 2nd century B.C. - 2nd century A.D. The Island in the Tiber (Isola Tiberina), where the river bends between the hills, on its left bank, Capitoline, Palatine and Aventine and on the right bank the Janiculum, offered the easiest crossing-point of the river; right from its origins, settlements clustered nearby, where the main route from the Etruscans in the north crossed the river in the direction of the Greeks in the south. This was the site of the Forum Boarium and the earliest river port dating from the 8th century B.C.; the earliest wooden bridge over the Tiber, called Pons Sublicius, was built on this fording point, later it was replaced by the **Ponte Emilio** or **Ponte Rotto**, the oldest stone bridge in Rome. The piers are of travertine and were built in 179 B.C.: the arch is sixteenth century; the bridge was viable until 1598 when it collapsed. The Tiber Island was later connected to the mainland by two bridges, the Cestio (46 B.C.) on the right bank, almost entirely rebuilt in the nineteenth century, and the **Ponte Fabricio** (also known as Ponte dei Quattro Capi) built in 62 B.C., with two wide spans and an opening in the central pier to take the thrust of the waters when the river was in flood. About 10 bridges crossed the Tiber within the walled city during the imperial epoch but only three remain: the two mentioned above, and the **Ponte Elio** built by Hadrian in 134 A.D. to link his tomb with Campus Martius of which the three central spans are now incorporated into Ponte Sant'Angelo. **Ponte Milvio or Molle**, built in 109 B.C., restored in the fifteenth century, was the bridge where the Via Flaminia, the Cassia, the Clodia etc. all crossed the Tiber: the four arches in the middle are the original ones.

The Roman **aqueducts** with their enormous structures were even more daringly conceived than the bridges. As the territory of Rome grew, aqueducts were built at the same time as the great roads: the Aqua Appia (4th century B.C.), the Anio Vetus (early 3rd century B.C.) and the Aqua Marcia (late 2nd century B.C.) all brought

water from the Aniene valley to the city. The most dramatic remains of these aqueducts are those of the Aqua Claudia to the south of the city; fragments of other aqueducts can be seen within the walls (no. 1) since they supplied the baths in the city (nos. 20,21). The very same conduits were re-used centuries later to supply the Renaissance and Baroque fountains with water (no. 101). Water was also used by the Romans to provide entertainment: Augustus built the enormous lake Naumachia Augusti in the year 2 B.C. in Trastevere in the area of Piazza Mastai; the Aqua Alsietina aqueduct was built expressly for this, and was later used for Aqua Paola (1610). Another important achievement of Roman engineering was the sewage system: the most important remains of these underground conduits to be seen is the end of the Cloaca Maxima which runs into the Tiber just below the Ponte Emilio.

Top, Ponte Fabricio, immediately above, Ponte Rotto (Emilio); opposite page: top, Ponte Milvio (Molle); below left, constructional detail of a Roman aqueduct by Piranesi; below right, Remains of the Acquedotto Claudio; bottom left, plan of the main Roman aqueducts (from Staccioli's, «Roma entro le Mura»).

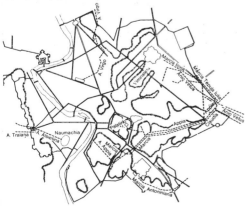

The architecture of power. Architecture, the art form in which the Romans excelled, was principally used (and in the most spectacular way possible) to celebrate power of the emperor, of a head of state who, following the oriental tradition, rose to become a god. The forum was not only the centre of public life with its temples, basilicas and libraries, but also a monument to the person of the emperor who was celebrated in equestrian statues, columns, obelisks and triumphal arches. Just as magnificent were the imperial residences such as Nero's Domus Aurea and those of Domitian and Septimius Severus; the layout became more and more complex and magnificent, and the interior decoration of marble, metals, stuccoes and frescoes, was of unprecedented splendour. The largest imperial palace was the one Diocletian built in Spalato (Split) in 300 A.D.: a complete citadel in which all the functions of power were concentrated. It became a model for the imperial residences of Byzantium, and subsequently influenced the urban concepts behind places such as St. Mark's Square in Venice and the Kremlin in Moscow.

View of the Roman Forum looking towards the Campidoglio.

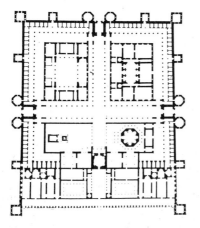

Emperor Theodosius the Great (379-395), with his court, on the balcony of the imperial palace of Constantinople, overlooking the Hippodrome (bas-relief at the base of the column of the Hippodrome, Istanbul); below, plan of Diocletian's palace at Spalato (Split).

4

THE ROMAN FORUM, 1st century B.C. - 4th century A.D. The valley to the north of the Palatine hill, adjoining the Campidoglio to the west, had been drained and paved by 600 B.C.: it was to become the hub of the city that was developing on the surrounding hills. During the republic, buildings and great temples rose around this space, the first forum, but it was not until the second and first centuries B.C., particularly under Caesar, that the Roman Forum became the monumental centre we see today; the whole area can be considered as a single architectural organism. It was in the first century B.C., with the Tabularium (Record Office) and the two great basilicas Aemilia and Julia, that Roman civil architecture established itself with prototypes that were to have such a fundamental influence on the whole development of western architecture. The **Tabularium** was erected in 79 B.C. against the steep hillside of the Campidoglio on a base of blocks of tufa, 73 metres long — a dramatic backdrop to the west end of the Forum. The Tabularium (where the state records were housed) consisted of a ground floor of 10 arches supported by Doric half-columns of marble (the first example of a motif that was to become widely used), behind which was a gallery; the first floor had a portico supported by Corinthian columns. On either side of the square stood the Curia and the Basilica Aemilia to the north, and the Temple of Saturn and the Basilica Julia to the south; monuments in front of the Tabularium included the Rostra, a platform 3 metres high and 24 metres long of tufa blocks forming the tribune for orators addressing the Comitium (44 B.C.). To one side of the Rostra, in front of the Arch of **Septimius Severus** (no. 8), stood the «Um-

Temple of Antoninus and Faustina, 2nd century.

Temple of Romulus, 4th century.

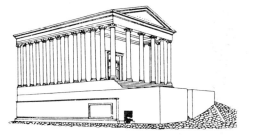

Above left, Reconstruction of the Temple of Saturn, Ist century B.C.; above right, Reconstruction of the Tabularium, 79 B.C.; below, Reconstruction of the Basilica Giulia, Ist. Century B.C. (all from Staccioli's «Roma entro le Mura»).

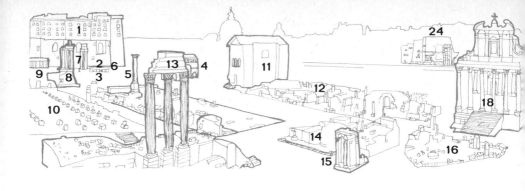

Main buildings in the Roman Forum.
1. Tabularium (and Palazzo Senatorio on the Campidoglio).
2. Rostrums.
3. Miliarium Aureum.
4. Arch of Septimus Severus.
5. Foca's Column.
6. Temple of Concord.
7. Temple of Vespasian.
8. Temple of Saturn.
9. Portico of the Dei Consenti.
10. Basilica Julia.
11. Curia.
12. Basilica Emilia.

bilicus Urbis», the symbolic centre of the capital; close by was the Milliarium Aureum (no. 1). In the centre of the square stands the Column of Phocas, built in honour of the Eastern emperor in 608, the last monument to be built in the Forum. Between the Rostra and the Tabularium there are fragments of three religious buildings, the Temple of Concord, three slender columns of the Temple of Vespasian (81 A.D.) and the low colonnade of the Porticus Deorum Consentium (367 A.D.), the last monument devoted to paganism built soon after of Julian the Apostate. The splendid ruins of the **Temple of Saturn** — eight granite Ionic columns of the portico which had a high travertine base — stand to the south. It was one of the most sacred monuments at the beginning of the republican era (erected 497 B.C. rebuilt in 42 B.C. and restored in the 3rd century A.D.); also known as the Aerarium, it housed the State treasures.

Close to the Temple of Saturn stands the **Basilica Julia**, the most impressive building in the Forum (101 × 49 metres), but little remains of this. It was started by Caesar (55-44 B.C.) and completed by Augustus, and consisted of a large hall surrounded by two double rows of porticoes with two storeys of arches supported by Doric half-columns. On the opposite side of the square, near to the other great basilica, the Aemilia, stands almost intact the **Curia** or Senate House:

its survival is due to the fact that it was transformed into a Christian church in the 7th century. According to tradition it was founded by King Tullus Hostilius, rebuilt by Caesar and again by Diocletian after a fire (284 A.D.); it consists of a large hall (18 × 27 m.) with an inlaid floor reconstructed from original materials, surrounded by steps where the 300 senators had their seats. The main door of the façade which once had a portico with columns, is of bronze, a copy of the original (now in S. Giovanni in Laterano where Borromini used it). The Forum square had three important religious buildings on the eastern end dedicated to the Dioscuri, to Caesar and to Augustus: little remains of them now.

The temple, dedicated to the twin sons of Jove and Leda, Castor and Pollux, the Dioscuri who were worshipped by the Romans, was founded in 484 B.C. and rebuilt under Augustus. It has the form of a peripteral temple with 8 columns along the front and sides. Nearby along the Via Sacra stands the Regia, seat of the Pontifex Maximus, the circular Temple of Vesta (191 A.D.) and the House of the Vestals (64 A.D.); this is built round a large courtyard 69 metres long. To the north of the Via Sacra the buildings are in a better state of preservation: the **Temple of Antoninus and Faustina**, built after the death of Faustina, wife of the Emperor Antoninus Pius, in 141 A.D.: it is almost intact thanks to its having been used as a

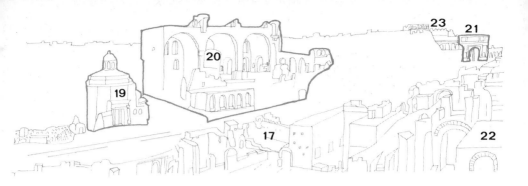

13. Temple of the Dioscuri.
14. Temple of Caesar.
15. Temple of Vesta.
16. Regia (residence of the Pontiflex Maximus).
17. House of the Vestals.
18. Temple of Antonius and Faustina.

19. Temple of Romulus.
20. Basilica of Maxentius.
21. Arch of Titus.
22. Remains or the Imperial Palaces on the Palatine hill.
23. Colosseum.
24. Fori Imperiali.

Christian church. Raised on a high platform the pronaos has 10 monolithic columns of Greek marble, cipolin, 17 metres high; the cell is well preserved up to the trabeation which is decorated with an elegant frieze of gryphons and candelabras. Close by is the so-called **Temple of Romulus**, dedicated to the son of Maxentius who in 309 died young and was deified; alternatively it might be the Temple of the Penates, brought here in the 4th century. It is a circular brick building covered by a cupola, with a concave façade, the door is decorated by two porphyry columns: the one we see is the original in bronze, and its lock is still in working order. Further along the Via Sacra tower are the vast brick remains of the **Basilica of Maxentius**, one of the mightiest buildings in Rome, founded by the Emperor Maxentius in the 306-312 and completed by Constantine who made a new entrance onto the Via Sacra (the main entrance faced the Colosseum). What we now see is part of the northern nave and apse: the arcade with its barrel vault 20.5 wide and 24.5 high decorated by lacunar motifs, inspired many Renaissance buildings. The original building had 3 naves (80 × 60 m.), the central one being of cement with a cross vault. The Forum ends as it began with a triumphal arch, that of **Titus** (no. 8).

Basilica of Maxentius.

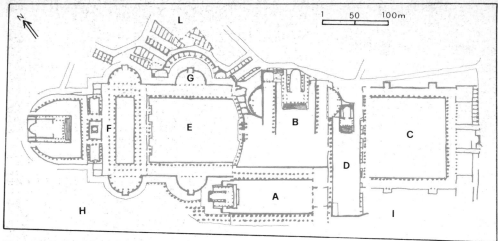

Plan of the Fori Iperiali:

A. Caesar's Forum.
B. Augustu's Forum.
C. Temple of Peace or Vespasian's Forum.
D. Nerva's Forum.
E. Trajan's Forum.

F. Trajan's Column.
G. Trajan's markets.
H. Campidoglio.
I. Roman Forum.
L. Quirinale.

5

THE IMPERIAL FORA, 1st century B.C. - 2nd century A.D. The Imperial Fora, built in a relatively brief period between the late first century B.C. and the early second century A.D. — a mere century and a half — form a complex of five squares laid out between the Capitoline and Quirinal hills, to the north of the Forum Romanum, of which they were the continuation. The squares were all connected and constituted the monumental heart of the capital, the true centre of imperial power, symbolised here in its most sumptuous and spectacular forms. Little remains of all this glory today and some of the fragments have been buried under the Via dei Fori Imperiali, cut to link Piazza Venezia and the Colosseum during the thirties in the Fascist period: moreover the road divides the area (600 × 300 metres) into two separate zones, making it difficult to decipher the remains of this archeological park. The earliest of these **fora** was planned by Caesar (54-46 B.C.), the **Forum Julium** was the model for the others: a long narrow square (160 × 75 metres) surrounded by a portico, just to the north of the present day Curia. In the centre stood an equestrian statue of the Dictator, and, on the Campidoglio side, was the Temple of Venus Genetrix, the goddess mother to Aeneas and progenitor of the Julian people. Soon after, between 31 and 2 B.C., **Augustus** built his Forum (now on the other side of the Via dei Fori Imperiali); nearly square (125 × 118 metres), it

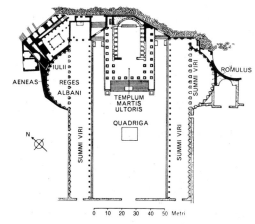

Plan of Augustu's Forum (from Staccioli's «Roma entro le Mura»).

Trajan's Column (detail), 107-112 A.D.

contained the Temple of Mars Ultor (Mars the Vindicator of Caesar's murderers) between two great exedrae; some important remains of this can be seen from Trajan's Market. Near the Temple was a great square hall containing the colossal statue of Augustus, 14 metres high. Before the building of the third forum, that of Nerva or Forum Transitorium, Vespasian erected the Temple of Peace, often called **Vespasian's Forum** mistakenly, in 71-75 A.D. to commemorate his victory over the Jews (it housed the spoils of the Temple of Jerusalem).

Near the Temple of Peace were marble slabs with the «Forma Urbis» engraved on them — a large-scale plan of Rome (1/246) at the time of Septimius Severus 203-211 A.D. (now preserved in the Museo di Roma in Palazzo Braschi). Domitian began building his forum in the decade of the 90s: it is known as the **Forum of Nerva** who completed it in 98 A.D.; it is a long narrow rectangle (120 × 45 metres) of which only two columns remain, the so-called «Colonnacce»: it formed the connecting link between the two Imperial Fora and the gardens of the Temple of Peace and for this reason was known as Forum Transitorium.

Ten years later, between 107 and 112 A.D., **Trajan** constructed the largest forum of the capital, stretching from the Forum of Augustus to beyond Trajan's Column — 300 metres long and 180 wide. In order to make room for this enormous complex a ridge running from the Quirinal Hill to the Campidoglio was destroyed, as was a stretch of the Servian walls: in this way the area of the **fora** was joined to that of Campus Martius where the new parts of Rome were beginning to develop. On one side of the square the Market of

Trajan was built. This great project, the work of the architect Apollodorus of Damascus, consisted of a square with porticoes, with two exedrae on the long sides. In the centre was an equestrian statue of the Emperor, and three vast buildings stood on the far side from the Forum of Augustus: the Basilica Ulpia, the largest in the city (170 × 60), with its five naves, two Libraries (one for Latin texts, one for Greek) with Trajan's column between them, lastly there was the Temple dedicated to the god-Emperor surrounded by a horse-shoe shaped portico. The sole monument still intact is **Trajan's Column** standing between the twin churches of S. Maria di Loreto (no. 55) and the eighteenth-century one of SS. Nome di Maria. It is 29.77 metres high (100 Roman feet), the height of the ridge that was demolished, and consists of 18 drums of Carrara marble decorated by spiral bas-reliefs 200 metres long, illustrating scenes from the conquest of Dacia (modern Romania) with a total of 2500 figures. We see the Roman army not only in battle scenes, but also building bridges, camps and fortifications; the sculptor (who might have been Apollodorus of Damascus) expresses himself «with a freedom of invention, a wealth of detail and lively touches that make this work one of the finest examples of ancient art» (Bairati - Finocchi). A statue of the emperor stood on the summit of the column, but in 1587 it was replaced by one of St. Peter. Inside the base a golden urn containing Trajan's ashes had been placed. On either side of the column the remains of the libraries can be seen. Near the Forum, on the slopes of the Quirinal hill, the **Market of Trajan** were built, one of the most interesting monuments of ancient Rome, and which has come down to us al-

Remains of Trajan's Forum.

Trajan's Markets: the Great Hall; below, Exedra; bottom, Plan of the markets.

most intact, with its roads and shops — perhaps this too was the work of Apollodorus of Damascus. It is a semicircular brick building above which are tiers of terraces ascending the slope: as has been mentioned the Quirinal hill had been cut to make room for the Forum below. The exedra of the markets has a hall with its apse at either end: between these were the shops. One of the best preserved parts is the Great Hall on the third floor, rectangular in shape with two storeys of shops, six on each side: the doors have lintels of travertine with a square window above. The hall has a vaulted roof supported by travertine piers — it is both monumental and functional, a typical example of ancient Roman architecture, one of the best preserved interiors of the city.

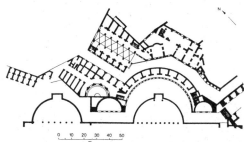

Remains of the Domus Augustana; below, plan of the imperial palaces.

6

THE IMPERIAL RESIDENCES ON THE PALATINE, 1st century B.C. - 2nd A.D. The Palatine Hill, about 50 metres high, rises from the flat area of the Forum Boarium, not far from the main fording-place across the Tiber around which the early settlements developed from the eighth century onwards: the traditional date for the founding of the city is 754 B.C. It was on this hill that the earliest fortified enclosure of the «Roma quadrata» stood; on the southern slope of the hill, traces of three early Iron Age huts have been found (9th century) on the site where the House of Romulus traditionally stood, not far from the Lupercal cave where legend has it that the basket containing Romulus and Remus was found: they had been transported by the river in flood. During the republic, the Palatine became a residential quarter for the wealthy: Cicero and Marcus Antonius as well as Augustus himself lived here before he became emperor. His private residence on the Palatine thus became the first imperial residence, and his example was followed by Tiberius, Nero and Domitian who built an enormous palace which was the imperial residence for centuries, until the byzantine period. The word «palace», meaning majestic residence, derives from the name of this hill; Palatine itself derives from Pales, the goddess of shepherds, in whose honour the Palilia, the celebration of the founding of the city, was held. Little remains of the imperial palaces, the ruins

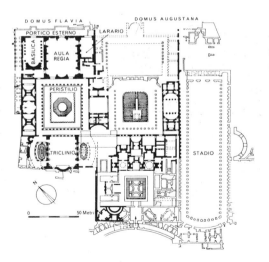

Remains of one of the fountains of the Domus Flavia, Ist century A.D.

Detail of a fresco in the House of Livia, Ist century B.C.

being overgrown with vegetation, «One feels as if one has strayed into the midst of a landscape by Claude Lorrain» as Georgina Masson remarked. This is the best place to understand the romantic taste for Roman ruins that inspired so many artists from the seventeenth century onwards, as well as the English landscape gardeners who filled their parks with «classical ruins» amidst the clumps of trees and artificial lakes. Today, the Palatine hill is almost entirely covered by the ruins of the vast palace of Domitian; to the west, however, are some important remains of the Domus Augustana built in 36 B.C., particulary the so-called House of Livia, wife of Augustus. The floors of three have been preserved, paved in black and white mosaic: the walls are decorated by lively paintings — those of the tablinium are particulary delightful — mythological scenes, «trompe l'oeil» doors and a kind of theatrical scene showing townscapes with elegant architectural perspective; we are reminded of the frescoes in the Venetian villas such as those of Veronese at Maser, probably inspired by this kind of Roman painting.

Little remains of the Domus Tiberiana, built by Augustus' successor: the site is now occupied by the sixteenth century Farnese gardens 'Horti Farnesiani'. **Domitian's Palace** was built between 81 and 96 A.D. by the architect Rabirius for the third emperor of the Flavian dynasty; it was the apotheosis of imperial residence, princely dwelling and royal palace. The building was divided into two parts, the Domus Flavia or Palazzo dei Flavi, where official ceremonies were held, and the Domus Augustana to the east which was the private residence of the imperial family. The **Domus Flavia** was built around a peristyle on one side of which was the Aula Regia or throne room, about 30 metres square, with walls decorated by niches and with an apse where the emperor sat. On the opposite side of the peristyle was the triclinium with its apse: part of the marble pavement decoration is still visible; the dining room looked out onto two nymphaeums with oval fountains (traces of the fountain on the right can be seen). Near the Aula Regia the so-called House of the Gryphons (dating from the republican period), decorated about the year 100 B.C., has been discovered; important remains include wall paintings (in a style midway between the first and second style of Pompei), stucco decorations (with gryphons facing each other) and a pavement of coloured marble with geometrical motifs. Of the other part of Domitian's palace, the **Domus Augustana**, very little remains; it was a building with at least two storeys, a semicircular portico facing south along the façade towards the Circus Maximus: to the west stood the **Stadium** or Hippodrome. It is 90 metres long with a two-storeyed portico along the side facing the Domus Augustana; a semicircular end may have housed the imperial platform (on one side, one of the two «metae» can still be seen). The oval enclosure at this end dates from the time of Theodoric (5th century), and was probably a riding school. At the end of the 2nd century, the Imperial Palace was enlarged by Septimius Severus who added the **Domus Severiana** on the south-east part of the hill. This enormous pile (which reminds us of Piranesi's prints) housed the baths, supplied by a conduit from the Aqua Claudia: Septimius Severus also built a large terrace, supported by huge brick arches.

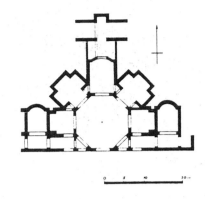

7

DOMUS AUREA, 64 - 68 A.D. The Domus Aurea
(Golden House) was built by Nero after the fire of
64 A.D., as his imperial residence and town
house, the work of the architects Severus and
Celer. It stood in the centre of an enormous park
(100 hectares) which stretched from the slopes
of the Palatine to those of the Esquiline and the
Coelian Hill — the flat land where the Colosseum
now stands. The palace itself was large (300 ×
90 metres) in three blocks: in the centre was a
pentagonal courtyard on one side of which was
the «Sala della Volta Dorata» (the room with the
gilded vault): it was decorated with golden stucco
work and mythological scenes painted by the artist Fabullus. The left-hand block had a large
peristyle, while that on the right was designed
round an **octagonal room**, covered by a cupola.
«Nero was influenced by oriental tradition and
probably wanted his residence to be 'The Palace
of the Sun'; oriental, too are the gardens and the
articulated plan of the buildings — not a single
monolithic block, but a series of constructions in
close contact with nature» (Argan). The Domus
Aurea was partly demolished and used for other
purposes by Nero's successors, being incorporated into the baths that Titus and, later, Trajan
built on the same site. The rooms are buried beneath later buildings and were not rediscovered
until the early sixteenth century when they were
described as «grottoes». The style of the wall
paintings, known as «grotesque», was a revelation to sixteenth-century artists, and inspired
Raffaello and his school.

Arch of Titus. 81 A.D.

Arch of Septimius Severus, 203 A.D.

8

TRIUMPHAL ARCHES, 1st - 4th centuries A.D.

Triumphal arches originated from the Hellenistic and Etruscan traditions of city gates, and became popular in Rome in the Augustan epoch. The three triumphal arches intact in Rome represent three different periods of Roman art, that of Titus, in the first century, that of Septimius Severus, in the 3rd century, and that of Constantine in the 4th. The **Arch of Titus** stands at the far end of the Forum Romanum at the end of the Via Sacra, (no. 4); it was built under Domitian, in 81 A.D. to commemorate the previous emperor, Titus' victory over the Jews (Titus was Domitian's brother). It was incorporated into a medieval fortress and was restored by Valadier in 1821 who rebuilt some damaged parts. It has a single arch (15.4 m. high and 13.5 wide, with a depth of 4.95 metres), its simple form could be called classical; it is decorated by cornices, half columns with composite Ionic-Corinthian capitals, used here for the first time, and friezes with a high attic bearing the inscription in elegant Roman letters. The underside of the arch has lacunar decoration and bas-reliefs showing Titus capturing Jerusalem: the style is more realistic than that of the Augustan period, but still classically balanced. The **Arch of Septimius Severus** is very different: it was built in 203 at the opposite end of the Forum Romanum in honour of the Emperor (it was the tenth year of his reign) and his sons Caracalla and Geta. It is much larger than the Arch of Titus (21 metres high, 23 wide and 11 deep), has three arches, surmounted by a high attic on which originally stood a quadriga with the figure of the emperor. Bas-reliefs above the side arches illustrate the victories of the Emperor and his sons over the Parthians and the Arabs.

The Arch of Constantine, near the Forum and the Colosseum, belongs to the late Roman period: it was built in 315 after Constantine's victory over Maxentius at the Milvian Bridge. It is double the size of Titus' arch (25 metres high, and over 30 wide), has three arches and is covered by reliefs many of which had been taken from earlier monuments «this operation is the first example of the systematic stripping of old buildings in order to make new ones, a process that has been going on up to the the modern age» (Straccioli). Reliefs from the reign of Constantine show symbolic characteristics (the likeness of the Emperor is shown face-on, much larger than all the other figures), which belong to the style of a later period. Some reliefs decorating this arch are the work of the maestro of Trajan's Column (no. 5) — pre-eminent in Roman art: eight statues of Dacians above the columns (the heads are not original), the two panels at the sides and those on the underside of the central arch. Another arch of the same period, the early 4th century, stands near the Forum Boarium, known as the **Arch of Janus**, a cubic structure with four equal sides, a cross vault which was probably crowned by a pyramid: it has 12 niches which once contained statues on all four sides.

Arch of Costantine, 315, A.D.

Detail of bas-relief on the Ara Pacis, 9 B.C.

Arch of Janus, 4th century A.D.

9

IMPERIAL MONUMENTS 1st century B.C. - 2nd A.D. If the triumphal arch can be described as a piece of architecture whose function is in part to provide surfaces for celebratory sculpture, other monuments such as columns and equestrian statues were originally conceived as works of sculpture in themselves: they become central elements of urban furniture, thanks to their position and dimensions. Perhaps the **Ara Pacis Augustae** is the most exemplarily didactic of Roman celebrative monuments: it was completed in the year 9 B.C. to commemorate the fact that peace reigned under Augustus throughout the empire, after the conquests of Gaul and Spain. It stood on the site of Palazzo Fiano in Via del Corso, in the Campus Martius; fragments of the altar came to light in the 16th century, and a thorough excavation of the site was made in 1938, when all the pieces were put together again. The reassembled altar now stands near the Tomb of Augustus (no. 13), not far from its original site. It consists of a marble screen (11.63 × 10.62 metres) surrounding an altar raised on a dais of steps. The sides of the screen facing outwards are covered with elegant reliefs illustrating the origins of Rome, a procession with the figures of Augustus and his family, and below these are fine scrolls of acanthus; the style is almost neo-classical, the expression of those ideals of control and magnificence of the Augustan period. The **Column of Marcus Aurelius** also in the Campus Martius, by the Via Lata, the first part of the Via Flaminia, now Piazza Colonna, was erected in 180 A.D. after the emperor's death. It was inspired by Trajan's column (no. 5) and is identical in size (29.6 metres high, diameter 3.7). The reliefs decorating it celebrate

43

The Column of Marcus Aurelius, 180 A.D.

Equestrian statue of Marcus Aurelius, 161-180 A.D.

the wars against the Germans and Sarmathians, and the style is quite different from that of Trajan's column, sculpted only eighty years before: it is simpler and more dramatic, a foretaste of the late Roman style. The only equestrian statue surviving (there were others in the Fora of Caesar and Augustus, no. 5) is that dedicated to **Marcus Aurelius** (161-180 A.D.) which probably came from a triumphal arch. In 1538 Michelangelo placed it in the centre of the Piazza del Campidoglio; it is the masterpiece of Roman bronze sculpture. Inspired by the famous monument to Alexander the Great: the emperor is portrayed speaking to his soldiers with a solemn gesture — a symbol of the power and grandeur of the State of Rome. For centuries this bronze sculpture has been the prototype of the equestrian statue.

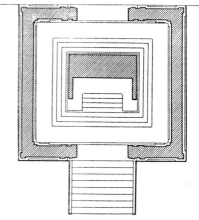

Plan of the Ara Pacis.

Temples and tombs. Temples, essential elements of the forum, and tombs can also be seen as expressions of power, at least during the imperial era. The Roman temple is derived directly from the Greek model, but developed characteristics peculiar to itself: it generally had a prostyle rather than a peripteral plan, thus enhancing the importance of the columns of the façade, raised on a dais. The two earliest temples in Rome, the Temple of the Fortuna Virilis and the Temple of Vesta, both date from the 2nd century B.C. and were probably the work of Greek architects. The Pantheon, instead, is the very symbol of Roman architecture, with the largest brick cupola ever built. Not far from Rome, at Palestrina, are the remains of one of the monuments most admired by Renaissance architects, the Sanctuary of the Fortuna Primigenia, dating from the late 2nd and early first century B.C.: the Helenistic inspiration is clear. Mithraic temples are also of interest, dedicated to the god Mithras: one of the largest is to be found in the Baths of Caracalla (no. 20). Pevsner reminds us that «the worship of Mithras, with its faith in a saviour, in sacrifice and rebirth was the most formidable rival to Christianity during the late Empire. It is no wonder, then, that the earliest form of the Christian church was identical with Mithraic temples». The great imperial tombs, the Mausoleums, also influenced Christian architecture, particularly the «martyria» of the first centuries, built on the place where a saint had been martyred or buried.

Temple of Fortuna Virile, 2nd century B.C.

Temple of Vesta, 2nd century B.C.

Axonometric view of the sanctuary of the Fortuna Primigenia at Palestrina, Ist century B.C. (from Quilici Gigli's «Roma fuori le Mura»).

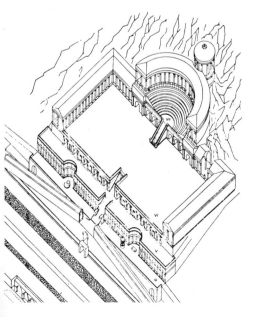

10

THE TEMPLES OF THE FORTUNA VIRILIS AND VESTA, 2nd century B.C. Near the Ponte Rotto (no. 3) in the Piazza della Bocca della Verità stand two early temples: the oldest is the **Temple of the Fortuna Virilis** probably dedicated to the god of the river port, Portunus. This is one of the earliest and best preserved of Roman buildings, dating from the late 2nd century B.C.; it was built on the Greek-Italic model, a raised dais, pronaos of four grooved Ionic columns of travertine and a rectangular **cella** of tufa with four half columns along each side. Originally both columns and half columns were covered with plaster which imitated marble. Nearby is the so-called **Temple of Vesta** dating from the late 2nd century B.C., probably dedicated to Hercules the Conqueror. It is circular in form and is the earliest marble building existing in Rome. The cylindrical **cella**, its door facing east, is surrounded by 20 grooved columns with Corinthian capitals, the work of a Greek architect, perhaps Hermodorus from Salamina. The roof is supported directly by the columns since both the trabeation and the original roof have disappeared.

11

ROMAN TEMPLES IN LARGO DI TORRE ARGENTINA, 4th - 1st centuries B.C. The excavations in Largo di Torre Argentina have brought to light four republican temples in the Campus Martius area, usually named A, B, C and D from right to left. They were restored by Domitian after the fire broke out in Campus Martius in 80 A.D.: the travertine pavement in front of the temples also dates from this period. Temple A, the second oldest, dates from 241 B.C., the period of the first Punic War. It consists of a hexastyle periptery with tufa columns raised on a dais — probably the result of rebuilding in the first century B.C. The two apses with traces of frescoes belonged to the medieval church of S. Nicola which was built into the ruins. Temple B, the most recent, called Temple of Fortune, 101 B.C., has a circular plan and was raised on a tufa platform. Subsequently enlarged, the **cella** incorporated the columns, making them seem like half columns. Temple C, the earliest, dates from late 4th — early 3rd centuries B.C.; it was raised on a podium and had columns on three sides. Temple D, much of it buried, dates from the early 2nd century, but was rebuilt a century later; it is raised on a podium with a flight of steps leading to a hexastyle pronaos.

12

PANTHEON, 118-125 A.D. The is one of the cardinal buildings in the history of European architecture: one of the largest temples of ancient Rome, and one which is still intact, having been transformed into a Christian church in the 7th century. The original temple was built by Agrippa in 27 A.D. and dedicated to «all the gods»: it was entirely rebuilt by Hadrian in 118-125 A.D. The temple has a circular **cella** covered by a vast cupola, and a large pronaos and tympanum on the north side. This pronaos, joined to the **cella** by a cubic brick structure, consists of 16 monolithic granite columns (12.5 metres high), eight of which on the façade have Corinthian capitals. The triangular pediment was once decorated by bronze reliefs. The bronze doors are probably original. The circular **cella** is a concrete cylinder (30 metres high and 6.2 thick) which takes the weight of the enormous hemispherical cupola, the largest ever constructed. This was originally covered with sheets of bronze, later replaced by lead; in the centre is a large opening or oculus, nearly nine metres in diameter, the only source of light in the building. «The interior of the rotonda is harmonious in its dimensions, the height of the **cella**, from the floor to the top of the dome, is equal to the diameter of the dome (43.3 metres); it is like a perfect sphere within a cylinder whose height is the radius of the sphere» (Straccioli). The interior has a semi-circular apse with six recesses, three on each side, alternately rectangular and semi-circular, with grooved columns of yellow marble. The cupola is decorated by five bands of coffering; the floor has been restored in the style of the original using the same marbles employed in the rest of the Pantheon (porphyry, granite, yellow marble).

Interior of the Pantheon.

Section from Palladio's «Quattro Libri», 1570.

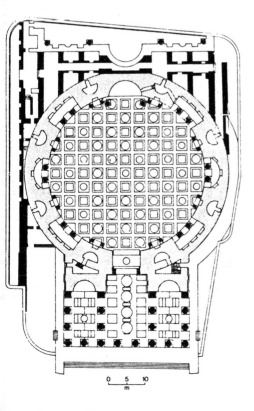

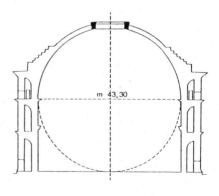

m 43,30

Ground plan and section (from Staccioli's «Roma entro le Mura»).

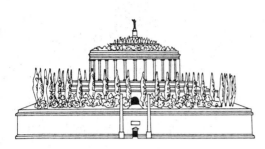

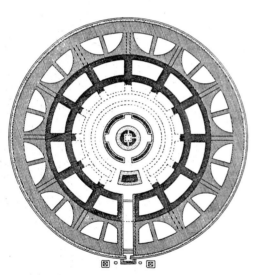

Mausoleum of Augustus: above left, Reconstruction; Above right, as it is today, below left, ground plan.

13

MAUSOLEUM OF AUGUSTUS, late 1st century B.C. The Mausoleum of Augustus, built by the first emperor as a tomb for himself and members of his family, stands in Piazza Augusto Imperatore near the Ara Pacis (no. 9). The monument underwent various vicissitudes over the centuries and was finally restored in 1936. It consisted of a square base with a circular edifice, covered with a conical mound of earth planted with cypresses and a statue of the emperor on top (diameter 87 metres, 44 in height). It was influenced by tombs of Greek kings, especially that of Alexander the Great, as well those of the Etruscans. On the south side the door was flanked by obelisks in the Egyptian tradition (now standing in Piazza del Quirinale and Piazza dell'Esquilino). Inside two circular corridors led to the round **cella**, in the centre of which was a square burial chamber housing the emperor's tomb. The Emperor's wife Livia, his son-in-law Agrippa, his stepson Drusus and his successors Tiberius, Caligula, Claudius and perhaps Vespasian and Nerva, were also buried in the mausoleum. [Piazza Augusto Imperatore].

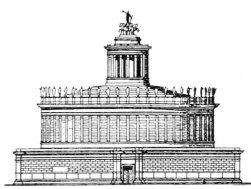

14

MAUSOLEUM OF HADRIAN, 130-139 A.D.

Hadrian's mausoleum, now known as Castel S. Angelo, is built to the same model as the Mausoleum of Augustus, and despite alterations and destruction, it has preserved its original structure better than that of Augustus. It, too, has a square base (89 metres each side), surmounted by a cylindrical edifice (64 metres in diameter and 21 in height) faced with travertine; the corner towers were added later in the late 15th century. The tomb was orginally covered by statues and vegetation growing in the earth mound: at the top there was probably a statue of the Emperor mounted on a quadriga. Inside, a curved ramp (125 metres long), in an excellent state of preservation, led to the burial chamber in the centre. Hadrian also built the Ponte Elio to connect his mausoleum with Campus Martius. All Roman Emperors from Hadrian to Caracalla were buried here. Aurelian incorporated it into his walls (270 A.D.). It underwent further alterations in the 11th, 15th and 16th centuries (when Julius II added papal apartments with a loggia). Despite all these modifications it is still one of the most impressive imperial buildings.

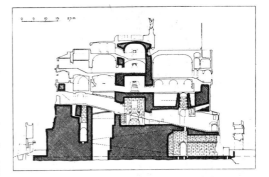

Hadrian's Mausoleum. Top left, as it appears today; top right, Reconstruction; Immediately above, section (all from Staccioli's «Roma entro le Mura»); below, Carpaccio, detail of «St. Ursula's Dream», 1495, Venice, Accademia Gallery.

15

TOMB OF CECILIA METELLA, late 1st century B.C. Cecilia Metella was the daughter of Quintus Metellus, the conqueror of Crete, and wife of Crassus, son of the triumvir; her tomb is the most famous monument on the Via Appia (no. 2), 3 kms from Porta S. Sebastiano. It was built at the end of the republican period, in the first century B.C., and consists of a cylindrical mausoleum (20 metres in diameter) faced with travertine which rests on a square base. At the top is a marble frieze decorated with bulls' skulls and garlands from which the name of surrounding area, Capo di Bove, comes. The funerary cell is high and narrow, ending with a conical vault. In Byzantine times it became a fortress, and subsequently was incorporated into eleventh-century fortifications. Nearby are the remains of the Circus of Maxentius, the temple of Romulus, son of Maxentius, and of the villa of the emperor himself. (306-312). [Via Appia Antica].

16

PYRAMID OF CAIUS CESTIUS, 12 B.C. The pyramid of Cestius, near the Porta Ostiense or S. Paolo, was built as the tomb of Caius Cestius Epulone, praetor and tribune, who died in 12 B.C. The pyramid stands on a travertine base and is faced with Carrara marble (29.5 metres wide and 36.4 high); inside is the burial chamber 4 × 6 metres with a painted vault. Coming from Via Persichetti the entrance has two corner columns: an inscription tells us that the tomb was built in 330 days. It is an original example of Augustian classicism, open to various exotic influences from Greece, the Orient and, in this case, from Egypt. Neo-classical artists, such as Canova, showed great interest in this monument. [Porta S. Paolo].

Detail of the frieze of Cecilia Metella's tomb, from an engraving by Piranesi.

Theatres, Amphitheatres and Baths. Roman theatres, too, are derived from Greek prototypes, although some modifications were made: the structure was no longer dictated by the lie of the land. A series of arches follow the curved cavea as can be seen in the theatre of Marcellus dating from the Augustan period, and even more spectacularly, in the Colosseum. The advanced construction technique and the hydraulic engineering which lie behind the creation of the baths is highly complex. Theatres, amphitheatres and baths were just as essential in Roman towns all over the known world as was the forum. These infrastructures for leisure activities, as they would now be called, exemplify aspects of the social habits of the ancient Romans similar to our own. The vast structures of the Colosseum, the Circus Maximus (2nd century B.C.), Domitian's Stadium (first century A.D.), now Piazza Navona, and the Anfiteatro Castrense (3rd century A.D.) still dominate the Roman townscape, although the buildings have been demolished to a great extent. Remains of another Circus, that of Maxentius (309 A.D.) stand on the Via Appia, near the Tomb of Cecilia Metella (no. 15).

17

TEMPLE OF MINERVA MEDICA, early 4th century A.D. Called Minerva Medica because of a statue of Minerva with a serpent (symbol of medicine) discovered here, this temple was probably the nympheum of the imperial villa of the Licini, built in the early 4th century. It consists of a brick hall with ten sides (25 metres diameter), once covered with a cement cupola (it collapsed in 1828). There are nine recesses on each side, with arched windows above, a typical example of Roman architecture influenced by the late Hellenist scenographic trends. This building was much admired by architects of the Renaissance and later periods: although modest in size, it is one of the most important ancient Roman buildings. [Via Giovanni Giolitti].

Roman theatre of El Djem, Tunisia.

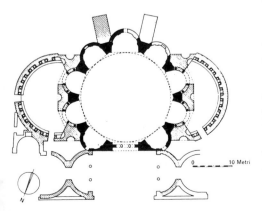

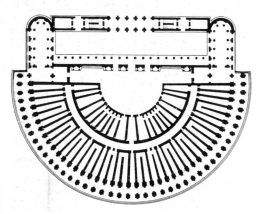

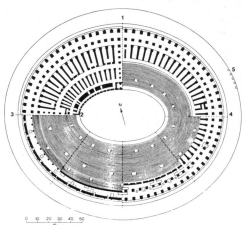

18

THEATRE OF MARCELLUS, 13 - 11 B.C. The remains of the Theatre of Marcellus stand between the slopes of the Campidoglio and Ponte Fabricio, incorporated into Palazzo Orsini, built by the Savelli family. It was founded by Caesar and completed by Augustus in 13 - 11 B.C. who dedicated it to his nephew Marcellus who was to have succeeded him, but died young. The building was transformed into a fortress in the Middle Ages, finally becoming part of the palace Baldassare Peruzzi built for the Savelli family in 1523-27. The original façade of the theatre had two orders of 41 arches each: today only twelve of them remain: pilasters with Doric half columns on the ground floor, and Ionic columns on the first floor; above there was probably an attic decorated by Corinthian pilasters making the total height of the building 35 metres. Inside, the cavea of the theatre had a diameter of 130 metres with a seating capacity of 15,000: almost nothing remains of this today. Behind the arches was a vaulted ambulatory, then the radial structure supporting the cavea partly in tufa and partly in cement with walls of «opus reticulatus». [Via del Teatro di Marcello].

19

COLOSSEUM, 72-80 A.D. The Flavian Amphitheatre, known as the Colosseum since medieval times, is the largest and most famous building of Ancient Rome, becoming the very symbol of the city. It was built on the marshy ground where the lake of the Golden House (no. 7) had stood between the Palatine and Esquiline Hills. «For the first time, a building had been conceived on an urban scale, related to the monumental area of the city» (Argan). It was founded in 72 A.D. by Vespasian and completed by his son Titus eight years later: the inauguration was celebrated by 100 days of events (gladiator fighting, capturing wild beasts, etc.). Like the Theatre of Marcellus, the exterior consisted of arcades with half-columns of all three orders (Doric, Ionic and Corinthian) crowned by an attic with Corinthian pilasters; the internal structure is far more vast and complex. Travertine was used to face the exterior, tufa inside with cement for the vaults; the stone blocks were fixed by metal cramps weighing altogether over 300 tons. There were 80 entrances, all numbered to facilitate access to the cavea; the entrance on the north east side is larger than the others and de-

corated by a porch and led to a hall decorated with stucco work, hence, in all probability, to the imperial box. The attic had a series of corbels used to fix wooden masts which supported the awning protecting spectators from the sun. The building is in the form of a helix (188 × 156 metres) and is 48.5 metres high: the actual area measures 76 × 46 m. The auditorium was divided into three sectors: the first and second had marble steps whereas the third sector, separated from the first two by a high wall, had steps in wood for seating; at the very top there was a terrace for standing room. The total capacity of the Colosseum was between 50,000 and 70,000 spectators. Below the arena were cells used to house the animals and equipment for the entertainments. It was in use until 523 under Theodorus when it was turned into a fortress; in 1312 the Emperor Henry VII gave it back to the Senate and the Roman people. For centuries it was used as a quarry for building materials (Palazzo Venezia, the Cancelleria, Porto Ripetta, etc.), but, despite this, it is still perfectly intelligible in all its greatness.

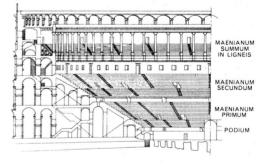

MAENIANUM SUMMUM IN LIGNEIS

MAENIANUM SECUNDUM

MAENIANUM PRIMUM

PODIUM

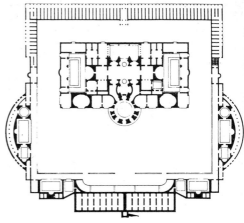

20

BATHS OF CARACALLA, 212-217 A.D. The Baths of Caracalla or Antoniane are the most magnificent thermal establishment left to us by ancient Rome (Diocletian's baths were larger but have been largely destroyed or rebuilt). They were built by Caracalla between 212 and 217, and were still functioning in 537, three centuries later when the Goths destroyed the aqueducts supplying Rome. Together with the Colosseum, these baths are perhaps the most impressive ancient monument of the capital. The enormous building, similar in plan to the Baths of Trajan, was surrounded by a large walled park (337 × 328 metres). The entrance was on the northeast side, with a portico: on the opposite side, behind the stadium, was an enormous cistern with a capacity of 80,000 cubic metres, divided into 64 cells, supplied by the Aqua Marcia conduit. The other two sides had a large exedra in the centre with a portico, the whole building measured 220 × 114 metres. The first room we see was the last to be used in the bathing process, the **frigidarium**, with its large swimming pool, then we come to the **tepidarium**, an enormous hall (58 × 24 metres) with side rooms leading to the palestrae or gymnasium; this hall had cross vaulting supported by eight pillars. We then go through a smaller **tepidarium**, then to the **calidarium**, a circular room 34 metres in diameter covered by a cupola, now destroyed: the calidarium is now used as the stage for outdoor performances of opera in the summer. All the

rooms were magnificently decorated with marble, statues and mosaics: some parts of the mosaic floor are the only decorations which have survived. It is thought that over 1,600 people could use the baths at a time; the hydraulic engineering and heating systems were the state of the art in ancient Rome. The Mithraic temple is of considerable interest, the largest discovered in Rome (20 × 40 metres), built underground along the north-west wall, near the big exedra; in the third century, oriental influences were affecting religion. [Via delle Terme di Caracalla].

Plan of the Temple of Mithras.

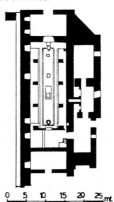

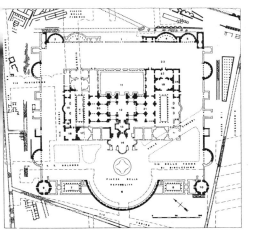

21

BATHS OF DIOCLETIAN, 298-306 A.D. Diocletian's baths, built between 298 and 306, were the largest in Rome, hence in the whole of the Roman world; today it is difficult to understand their design, much has been demolished and many alterations made (Piazza Esedra, Church of S. Bernardo, Church of S. Maria degli Angeli, Museo delle Terme, etc.). The outer wall (380 × 365) ran from Via Volturno, where the entrance was, to Piazza Esedra which follows the exedra on the south-west side, probably used for theatrical performances. At the south corners of the wall were two circular rooms, one of which has been transformed into the sixteenth-century church of S. Bernardo, with the fine cupola (22 metres diameter), resembling a small Pantheon (no. 65). The bath establishment (250 × 180 metres) could accommodate 3000 people at one time; part of it has been incorporated into the church of **S. Maria degli Angeli**. Michelangelo transformed the tepidarium into a church in 1561: the brick façade was one of the apses of the **calidarium**. Vanvitelli made further alterations to the church in the eighteenth century: he enlarged the apse, taking in part of the **frigidarium**. The nave of the church (27 × 90.8 metres) with its three large cross vaults (28 metres high), and the eight huge monolithic columns of red granite (13.8 metres high) both respect the original structure of the bathing hall. Together with the Pantheon it is the most splendid of ancient interiors, and one of the best preserved: it certainly influenced Bramante and Michelangelo when they built S. Pietro, as well as Palladio in designing his country houses and his churches. The Museo delle Terme occupies a series of large halls in the eastern part of the **tepidarium** and **frigidarium**. [Piazza della Repubblica].

Michelangelo, S. Maria degli Angeli. Top left, Plan of the baths; top right View of the nave, the former tepidarium; below, Ground plan of the church (from Staccioli's «Roma entro le Mura»).

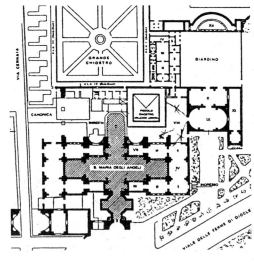

Christian architecture, the most important artistic expression of the medieval period, has its origins in the late imperial era under Constantine. The earliest Christian buildings echo classical models: firstly, the basilica, the meeting house of the community (in pagan temples, the worship took place outside the building, only the priest could enter the **cella** inside); the mausoleum, circular buildings, used for burial places or a monument to a martyr (martyrium), or as baptisteries. These two types of construction were to be the architectural models for Christian buildings — particularly in Rome — reproduced with slight variations over the following centuries. The Roman bishops, spiritual heads of the whole of Christianity, consciously emphasised their antique origins, thus distinguishing themselves from other political-religious centres both in the East and West, especially Byzantium. After the fall of the Western Empire (476), Rome became a mere Byzantine province, losing all its importance, even though the papacy was still considered the sole authority of the Latin world, not only religious but also in a sense political. Over the centuries the population of Rome continued to decrease — of the million inhabitants of the imperial period, only some tens of thousands were left when the papacy was moved to Avignon.

Early-Christian and pre-Romanesque architecture (4th - 5th centuries). The Emperor Constantine the Great (306-337) was one of the great builders of ancient Rome: he built baths on the Quirinal, the triumphal arch near the Colosseum (no. 8), he completed the basilica of Maxentius in the Forum (no. 4) and restored the Circus Maximus; all this activity can be seen as a preparation for his magnum opus, the creation of a new imperial capital on the Bosphorus, Constantinople, founded in 324. Constantinople was built with Rome as its model, with the imperial palace, the hippodrome, the Forum with its column and, close by, the cathedral of St. Sophia, rebuilt by Justinian two centuries later. Inside the city walls, Constantine built his own mausoleum, the church of the Twelve Apostles. The City was to be the apotheosis of a Christian capital, as Krautheimer observes, «an offering to Christ who had given Constantine the victory over Licinius». The Emperor was having his own back on Rome where he had encountered obstacles to the building of the early churches — the Lateran basilica, seat of the Bishop, and the churches dedicated to St. Peter and St. Paul soon after the Edict of Tolerance of 313. These churches were built far from the centre of the city, on land owned by the Emperor himself; evidently Constantine could not and would not offend the susceptibilities of the Senate and the prominent families still loyal to the pagan divinities (in 367 the Porticus Deorum Consentium, was erected in the Forum, the last pagan monument to be built). From the 5th century onwards, Rome was completely converted to Christianity — there were already 25 **tituli** or parishes. Many important Christian churches were being erected, apart from the basilicas of Constantine, such as S. Costanza (no. 22), S. Stefano Rotondo (no. 24), S. Maria Maggiore (no. 25), S. Sabina (no. 26) etc. These churches were based on the basilica form — the hall where justice was administered: thus the figure of Christ appears in the apse (e.g. S. Pudenziana no. 30) «as a **basileus** (King) on his throne, his hand raised in a gesture of **adlocutio** (addressing his subjects) dressed in purple robes and cloth of the emperor, flanked by apostles dressed like senators» (Krautheimer). These churches were characterised by sober, classical architecture which was very different from the sumptuous constructions of the late imperial period: the Christian buildings exemplify the contrast between the «subtle theory of proportion and the brutal rhetoric of mere dimension» as Argan remarks. While Rome was decaying, Constantinople was becoming the most splendid city of the empire, thanks to Justinian (527-565) who, in the 6th century, built splendid monuments on the Bosphorus and in Ravenna, the capital of Byzantine Italy. In Rome, on the other hand, the influence of Byzantium is marginal: exceptions are the elegant mosaics decorating the apse of S. Agnese (no. 27) and those of the chapel of S. Zenone in the church of S. Prassede (no. 30).

S. Pietro's Basilica before the XVth century rebuilding.

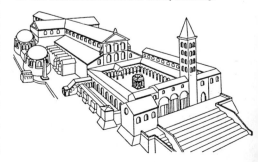

22

MAUSOLEUM OF S. COSTANZA, 4th century.
Built by Constantine around 320 as a
mausoleum for his daughter Costanza or Costantina, this is the earliest and most important
Early-Christian church with a central plan surviving in Rome in the style of the pagan
mausoleums, the sarcophagus in the centre. It
was transformed into a church in the 13th century. The cupola (22.5 metres diameter) is supported by 12 pairs of granite columns in a double
ring, connected by trabeation and arches: a
strong clear structure which leads our interest to
the centre of the building, lit by the 12 windows in
the cupola. The circular ambulatory has a barrel-
vaulted ceiling decorated with mosaics on a
white background: the designs are geometrical
or floral with scenes of the grape harvest, a typical late imperial motif with a symbolic Christian
significance. The mausoleum is close to the
church of S. Agnese (no. 27), founded by the
same daughter of the Emperor, Costantina. [Via
S. Costanza].

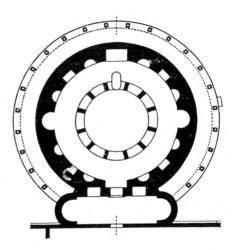

23

**BAPTISTERY OF S. GIOVANNI IN LATERANO,
4th - 5th centuries**. This is the earliest part of the
Lateran group of buildings, the Cathedral of
Rome where popes had their residence for over
10 centuries (no. 63), i.e. from the time of Constantine until they removed to the Vatican in the
15th century. Constantine built the baptistery,
probably on the site of a nymphaeum of the Lateran Palace: it was altered a century later by pope
Sixtus III (440), this is the structure we see today.
It was inspired by classical models, the prototype
of all later baptisteries, such as the baptistery of
Florence which was probably also built in the 5th
century. It has an octagonal plan, with a central
pool used for baptism by immersion: eight porphyry columns support an architrave, also octagonal in form (this bears an inscription exalting
baptism). Above the architrave white marble columns support the dome. Surrounding the Baptistery are four chapels of different periods: that of
S. Rufina, the original narthex transformed in the
12th century, in the apse is a 5th century mosaic
with acanthus scrolls; another chapel is dedicated to St. John the Baptist (5th century) with
early bronze doors; the chapel of S. Venanzio
(7th century) and the chapel of St. John the
Evangelist (5th century) with mosaics of the
same period and bronze door of the 12th century.
(For the cloister, the basilica and the palace, c.f.
nos. 33 and 63).

24

S. STEFANO ROTONDO, 5th century. This is a
circular early-Christian church built on the Celio
Hill between 468 and 483. It was probably inspired by the church of the Holy Sepulchre in
Jerusalem, it has undergone various modifications over the centuries. It has a circular inner
area surrounded by two concentric ambulatories
with Ionic columns supporting the high tambour.
The outer colonnade is interrupted by the entrances to the four chapels, forming a Greek cross
inscribed within a circle. The entrance portico
and the interior arches supporting the wooden
ceiling are 12th century additions. During the restoration by Alberti in 1453, the outer ring of columns and three arms of the Greek cross were
demolished. The outer wall was decorated by
16th century frescoes with scenes of Christian
martyrdom. [Via S. Stefano Rotondo].

25

S. MARIA MAGGIORE, 5th century. S. Maria Maggiore is the earliest patriarchal basilica in Rome, after those of S. Giovanni in Laterano, S. Pietro and S. Paolo, built under Constantine, and the only one to have preserved the original structure. It was founded by Pope Liberius (352-66) and rebuilt by Sixtus III (432-40) after the Council of Ephesus in 431 which recognised the cult of the Virgin, Mother of Christ. This was the first Christian basilica to be erected in the centre of the city, unlike Constantine's eccentric ones; it is a typical early-Christian church on the plan of the ancient classical basilicas, with a vast central nave divided from two side naves by two rows of Ionic columns supporting the architraves. The walls are decorated by 36 mosaic panels dating from the 5th century in the classical style; the apse was rebuilt in the 13th century and decorated by mosaics by Torriti (1295). The Cosmatesque pavement is 12th century, and the magnificent lacunar ceiling (late 15th century) is attributed to Giuliano da Sangallo. The Romanesque bell-tower (14th century) is the highest in Rome (75 metres).

From the late 16th century, in the time of the Counter-Reformation when the worship of the Virgin was flourishing, the basilica was enlarged by buildings which completely transformed the exterior aspect: **the Sforza chapel**, originally designed by Michelangelo, but built by Giacomo della Porta (1564-73); the **Sistine chapel** built by Domenico Fontana (1585) for Sixtus V Peretti; the **Pauline chapel** built by Flaminio Ponzio (1611) for Paolo V Borghese. This is a sumptuous piece of Baroque decoration with works in precious marble, stucco and bronze by Camillo Mariani, Pietro Bernini, the father of Lorenzo, and others, the frescoes are by Cavalier d'Arpino, Cigoli, Guido Reni, etc. The exterior of the **apse**, with a flight of steps was designed by Carlo Rinaldi in 1673, one of his most important works, while the **façade** with the great loggia was de-

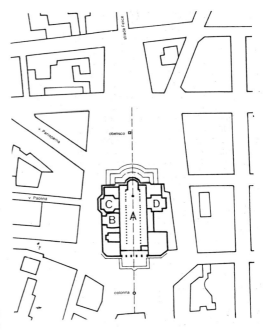

S. Maria Maggiore. Top left, Interior; top right, Detail of mosaics (Vth century) on the walls of the nave; above, Plan of the basilica: A. Nave; B. Sforza Chapel; C. Paolina Chapel; D. Sistine Chapel (from Insolera's «Roma»).

signed by Ferdinando Fuga in 1743, a late
Baroque masterpiece. On either side of the
façade are the twin palaces the Patriarchate, the
right-hand one dates from 1605 and the other is
much later, 1721-43. Thus the ancient early-
Christian basilica was enclosed within a series of
late 16th century and Baroque structures and
placed at the centre of an important road system,
emphasising both the religious and nodal aspect
in the pilgrims' road between S. Pietro and S.
Giovanni Laterano; this was perhaps the most
spectacular development of the popes in the
early Counter-Reformation period, between
1564 and 1643, making S. Maria Maggiore the
third great church of Rome. [Piazza S. Maria
Maggiore].

S. Maria Maggiore. Top View of the apse (Rainaldi, 1673) from
an engraving by Piranesi; above left, The façade (Fuga, 1743);
above right, Interior of the Paolina Chapel (Ponzio 1611).

S. Sabina. Left, Detail of the 5th-century wooden door; right, Nave.

26

S. SABINA, 5th century. S. Sabina, built on the Aventine Hill by Peter of Illyria between 422-432 A.D., contemporary with S. Maria Maggiore, seems to be the most authentic of Rome's early-Christian churches. Spacious, unadorned, luminous; it reminds us of the churches in Ravenna: here the columns are connected by arches instead of an architrave, for the first time. The geometric frieze of coloured marble between the arches and in the apse also dates from the fifth century. As Argan observes: «The church expresses its function soberly and clearly: this is the ideal site where spiritual harmony of the religious community corresponds to the harmony and limpidity of the forms defining the space. In open dissent with «imperial» architecture, form is opposed to force, the subtle theory of proportion to the brutal rhetoric of dimensions, the eternity of spiritual things to the stabilty of mere power». The wooden doors also dating from the fifth century are extremely interesting, both at an artistic level and for the subject matter — this is the very first piece of carving that illustrates the crucifixion. [Piazza Pietro d'Illiria].

27

S. AGNESE FUORI LE MURA, 7th century.
One of the best-preserved early-Christian
basilicas, it was founded in the early 4th century
by Constantia, daughter of Constantine the
Great along the Via Nomentana, on the site
where the martyr was buried: close by stands the
Mausoleum of S. Costanza (no. 25). The church
was later rebuilt by Pope Honorius I (625-638).
The name Agnese comes probably from
«agnus», meaning lamb, given to a young girl
whose name is unknown: she was courted by a
member of the imperial family, recognised as
being Christian, she was condemned to be burnt
to death; when she survived this, she was de-
capitated in 304. The church, preceded by the
narthex, has three naves divided by antique columns with Corinthian capitals, above which are
the women's galleries. The mosaics in the apse
(dating from the 7th century, and one of the finest
examples of Byzantine art in Rome), show S. Agnese, dressed like an empress, between the
Popes Symmachus and Honorius, the latter
holding a model of the church. [Via Nomentana].

28

S. MARIA IN DOMNICA, 9th century. Built on
the Celio Hill by Pope Paschal I (817-824), this
church expressed a different conception of
space from the naves of the other early-Christian
and Byzantine churches. Here we have an
enormously wide nave, giving the impression of
a single undivided space, emphasised by the
width of the shallow apse. The apse, framed by
two porphyry columns with Ionic capitals, holds
our attention with its superb 9th century mosaics:
the Virgin enthroned surrounded by multitudes of
angels, with Pope Pascal kneeling at her feet.
Above the apse are the 12 apostles round the
figure of Christ, supported by angels. The Renaissance façade with its portico is the work of
Andrea Sansovino (1513-14). [Piazza della
Navicella].

29

S. MARIA IN COSMEDIN, 8th century. Originally a 4th century oratory near the Forum Boarium which incorporated elements of an earlier Roman building, it was transformed into a church by Pope Hadrian I (772-95) and donated to the Greek colony, refugees from persecution by the Iconoclasts. Built on the basilica plan, divided into three naves by antique column and walls between them which differentiate it from the traditional early-Christian church. Zevi describes it as «a unique jewel of the silent genius of those centuries, where within the tradition, not justified by technical necessity, prompted solely by a new, timidly expressed spatial conception, an architect had the courage to break the rhythm». The church is decorated by a splendid 13th century cosmatesque decoration of the pavement, choir, ambo, paschal candlestick, episcopal throne and the altar canopy. The lovely Romanesque bell tower (12th century) is almost transparent, perforated as it is by innumerable mullioned windows. [Piazza Bocca della Verità].

30

S. PRASSEDE, 9th century. The church of S. Prassede, like that of S. Pudenziana, is close to S. Maria Maggiore; founded in the late 4th or early 5th century to honour the daughters of Senator Pudente with whom St. Peter lived in his house (on the same site as the church dedicated to S. Pudenziana, Prassede's sister). S. Prassede was rebuilt by Pope Paschal I (817-824) with a porch, a vestibule and an open atrium. The interior is on the basilica plan, with three naves, the central one very wide; the building has been much altered, its most interesting feature is the **chapel of S. Zenone** in the right-hand nave. This is the most important Byzantine monument in Rome, it looks as if it had been moved directly from Ravenna, dating from the 9th century. Paschal I built it for the mausoleum of his mother Theodora: it is a square chapel with a cross vault, entirely covered by mosaics — a perfect marriage of architecture and decoration. On the vault is the figure of Christ, with angels, inspired by the mosaics of Ravenna (6th century), while the Virgin and saints decorate the walls. The twin church of **S. Pudenziana**, although rebuilt in the 16th century, still has early mosaics dating from the original 4th century church, with the figure of Christ surrounded by the apostles against a background of the city of Jerusalem, a splendid piece of antique decoration. [Via S. Martino ai Monti].

Top left, Nave of S. Prassede; top right, Chapel of S. Zenone, 9th century; immediately above, S. Prudenziana (detail of the mosaic decoration, showing Christ with the apostles, 9th century).

From Romanesque to Gothic (11th - 14th centuries). The development of new building in cities all over Europe, from the 11th century onwards, produced new styles of architecture — Romanesque and later Gothic, and new types of buildings e.g. the public palace, symbol of a new kind of social organisation, that of the «Commune». Rome too acquired its own Commune in 1144, with the re-establishment of the Senate in the Campidoglio, but it functioned with difficulty. The papacy and local aristocracy could not tolerate any other power structures in their city. This is the reason why Rome had no real public hall: the only civic architecture surviving from this period is that of the towers, the remains of fortified houses built by the feudal barons (no. 40). The importance of the great religious orders — Franciscans and Dominicans — was restricted in Rome: in other cities they were some of the most important builders. Examples of Romanesque buildings in Rome are extremely limited while there is really only one Gothic church, that of S. Maria sopra Minerva (no. 37). Other churches continued to be built in the early-Christian tradition, e.g. S. Maria in Trastevere (no. 32). The 13th century — the period of transition from Romanesque to Gothic — saw an interesting flowering of artistic activity, especially in the fields of painting, mosaic and sculpture: a phenomenon similar to the «proto-Renaissance» developments at the court of Federik II, which left splendid works of art in cities as different as Venice and Pisa. The most important sculptor working in Rome in the 13th century did, in fact, come from Pisa, **Arnolfo da Cambio** (1245-1302); during the same period the elegant tradition of the Cosmati school of architects and mosaic craftsmen who used the ancient art of marble decoration in a new way flourished in Rome. These artists were so famous that in 1270, the King of England summoned one of them, Petrus Romanus, to build the tomb of Edward the Confessor in Westminster Abbey, the holy King who had founded the Abbey. Another artist, one the most influential painters of the 13th century, Pietro Cavallini (working from 1273-1308), also came from Rome: both in painting and in mosaics, he used a classical style in a modern way; we know that Giotto passed through Rome in his early years and saw Cavallini's work. When the popes moved to Avignon in 1305, all this artistic fervour was interrupted: they did not return to Rome until 1377; this hiatus is the most critical period for the city, and it was not until the end of the next century that artistic and architectural creativity flourished once more, and by then the Renaissance started to develop.

Romanesque bell-towers. From top to bottom: (1) S. Francesca Romana; (2) S. Giovanni a Porta Latina; (3) S. Silvestro in Capite.

S. Clemente. Top left, Nave; top right, Detail of mosaics in the apse (12th century); above, 11th-century fresco in the lower church.

31

S. CLEMENTE, 11th - 12th centuries. There are actually two churches, one on top of another, the earlier one (4th century) is the foundation for the church built by Pascal II, (1099-1118). Even the lower church was built over a pre-existing structure: it was built on the site of the house of Pope Clement I, the third pope after St. Peter (88-97). The upper church, despite eighteenth-century additions, preserves its original Romanesque 12th century aspect: naves divided by rows of seven antique columns, interrupted by a pilaster — similar to the plan of S. Maria in Cosmedin. The whole church is decorated in the Cosmatesque style — this is probably the most important and sumptuous interior carried out by these artists — the pavement of porphyry and serpentine, the choir, ambos and the pascal candlestick. The splendid mosaic in the apse also dates from the 12th century: it has early-Christian motifs (reminding us of the Lateran baptistery) illustrating the Triumph of the Cross. The figure of Christ is surrounded by scrolls of luxuriant foliage, creating a gloriously irridescent effect which enchanted that most elegant of the Viennese Secession painters, Gustav Klimt (perhaps these mosaics inspired the decoration of Palais Stoclet in Brussels). The chapel of S. Caterina in the left-hand nave is adorned with the famous frescoes of Masolino da Panicale (circa 1450). In the lower church (4th century), also with three naves (there is an adjoining Mithraic temple dating from the 3rd century), are preserved 11th century frescoes of the lives of St. Clement and of Sisinnus [Piazza S. Clemente].

32

S. MARIA IN TRASTEVERE, 12th century.
Traditionally founded by St. Calixtus in 221, it
was rebuilt by Innocent II (1130-43), and, despite
alterations and redecorations the interior still preserves its original aspect. The naves are divided
by 21 antique columns of granite, supporting a
trabeation similar to that of S. Maria Maggiore
(no. 25): this is a conscious echo of early-Christian features, a deliberate return to the past.
Pietro Cavallini's mosaics (circa 1291) are also
inspired by classical models: six panels between
the apse windows with episodes in the life of the
Virgin; the figures possess the dignity of antique
statues. The mosaics in the semi-dome of the
apse date from Innocent II. The church has a fine
12th century bell-tower; the Baroque portico was
added by Carlo Fontana in 1702. Even more
Baroque is the Avila Chapel in the left-hand
nave, the masterpiece of Antonio Gherardi
(1686) in the style of Borromini; in the cupola,
four angels appear to support the **lanterna** of yet
another cupola. In the nearby convent of **S.
Cecilia**, Cavallini's masterpiece can be seen, a
fresco of the Last Judgement, 1295. [Piazza di S.
Maria in Trastevere].

S. Maria in Trastevere. Top left, Apse; top right, Detail of mosaic
decoration of the apse by Pietro Cavallini (about 1291); immediately above, Detail of Pietro Cavallini's frescoes in the nearby convent of S. Cecilia (about 1293).

33
CLOISTER OF S. GIOVANNI LATERANO, 12th century. After the Baptistery (no. 23), the cloisters are the oldest part of S. Giovanni Laterano: they constitute one of the most magnificent achievements of the Cosmatesque school, having been built in 1215-1232 by two Vassallettos, father and son, as the inscription reminds us. The cloister arches are supported by twin columns of varying shapes, often decorated with mosaics; the capitals are equally varied and the frieze, too, is embellished by brilliant mosaics. Fragments of works from the medieval basilica are preserved in the cloisters — pieces of sculpture, tombstones, etc., including important reliefs from the tomb of Cardinal Annibaldi (who died in 1274), his sarcophagus stands in the nave on the far left, a masterpiece of Arnolfo da Cambio. (Basilica of S. Giovanni no. 64). [Piazza di S. Giovanni Laterano].

34
CLOISTER OF S. PAOLO FUORI LE MURA, 13th century. S. Paolo Fuori le Mura was the only one of Constantine's three basilicas remaining intact up to the last century, but it was almost completely destroyed by a fire in 1823, and rebuilt as a fairly faithful copy of the original. It has the clarity of a neoclassical building, and it is interesting for us to see a 19th century interpretation of an early-Christian basilica. The apse is the only original part: it preserves the 5th-century mosaics on the triumphal arch and, in the half-dome, Christ blessing with 4 saints, the work of Venetian mosaic artists (c. 1220), the same artists who were completing the decoration of S. Marco in that period. Above the high altar stands Arnolfo da Cambio's lovely canopy (1285) supported by porphyry columns with gold capitals, probably Pietro Cavallini had a hand in the design. The cloister was also saved from the fire in all its beauty, the work of the Vassallettos who built the cloisters in S. Giovanni Laterano (no. 33). Here, too, the twin columns are wonderfully varied — straight, twisted, octagonal, often decorated with mosaic; the architrave is enlivened by polychrome marbles. [Via Ostiense].

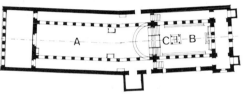

S. Lorenzo Fuori le Mura. Above left, Presbytery (6th century) shawing ciborium (12th century); above right, Façade and portico; left, Ground plan of the church: A Nave of the early church dedicated to the Virgin Mary: B the church of. S. Lorenzo; C the Ciborium; below, Cloister (12th century).

35

S. LORENZO FUORI LE MURA, 7th-13th centuries. Another typically Roman palimpsest, an early church beside a later one: there are two churches united into one, probably in the 13th century, when the two apses were demolished. The earlier church, dedicated to S. Lorenzo, founded by Constantine on the saint's burial place, was rebuill in the 6th century, while the church which forms the central nave, dedicated to the Virgin, dates from the 5th-8th centuries. The portico with six columns was added by Vassalletto in 1220, the trabeation is exquisitely decorated by mosaics; on the left-hand wall is Giacomo Manzu's monument to Alcide De Gasperi. The first church we enter, that dedicated to the Virgin, has 3 naves divided by ancient columns, with the pavement, ambos and pascal candelabra all in cosmatesque work (12th-13th centuries). The raised chancel is formed by the nave of the earlier church of S. Lorenzo — there are 10 fine fluted columns with composite capitals supporting the women's gallery. The elegant ciborium with a pyramid-shaped roof is the earliest example of cosmatesque work we have (1148). There is an interesting Romanesque cloister dating from the late 12th century, with single and twin columns — the only example in Rome of a cloister with an upper storey. [Via Tiburtina].

36

S. MARIA D'ARACOELI, 13th century. This is a very early church (7th century if not earlier), founded on the highest point of the Capitoline hill, on the spot where the Sibyl prophesied to Augustus the birth of Christ («Haec est ara filii Dei»), whence its name derives. It was a Benedictine abbey in the 10th century, it passed to the Franciscans in 1250, who built the present church in the Romanesque style with some Gothic elements — the chapel with pointed crossed arches. During the middle ages the cloisters of the convent were used as a meeting place for the city councillors. The simple brick façade dates from the early 14th century and is preceded by a flight of 122 steps built in 1348. The interior has three naves divided by columns taken from classical buildings. The cosmatesque pavement is 13th century, the pulpits were restored later. The splendid ceiling is a commemoration of the battle of Lepanto, 1571. On the wall where we enter stands the tomb of Giovanni Crivelli, archdeacon of Aquileia (died 1432), the work of Donatello. In the first chapel on the right are frescoes of the life of S. Bernardino of Siena, a masterpiece of Pinturicchio (c. 1486). [Campidoglio].

37

S. MARIA SOPRA MINERVA, 13th century. Founded in the 8th century on the site of the temple of Minerva Calcidica, this church was rebuilt by the Dominicans in 1280 in the Gothic style: it is the only Gothic church in Rome. The plans were said to have been the work of the friars Sisto and Ristoro, who built the church of S. Maria Novella in Florence. The interior with three naves and cruciform pilasters, despite the 19 c. decoration, still has that severe monumental quality typical of Italian Gothic architecture. Among the many works of art which have accumulated over the centuries, the most important are the Carafa chapel, decorated with frescoes of Filippino Lippi, and, to the left of the high altar, Michelangelo's «Christ bearing the Cross» (1521). Like many other conventual churches, it was the burial place of important figures: S. Caterina di Siena (died 1380), Beato Angelico (died 1455), the famous Dominican painter, and Cardinal Pietro Bembo, the great humanist (died 1547). [Piazza della Minerva].

38

CASA DEI CRESCENZI, 11th-12th centuries.
This is an interesting example of an eleventh-century house belonging to the Crescenzi, one of the most powerful families in Rome at this time: it stands near the Forum Boarium, commanding the crossing-place of the Tiber. The building is a sort of **collage** of fragments of classical buildings, displayed as if to ennoble the brick architecture; an inscription on the façade declares that it was built «to renew the ancient splendour of Rome», in the same spirit noticeable in the religious architecture of the period e.g. S. Maria in Trastevere, (no. 32). The arch over the doorway is part of the cornice from a classical building, while the other façade has a series of half-columns with parastas with brick capitals supporting late Roman corbels, and, over the architrave, more corbels supporting the overhanging first floor of which only fragments remain. [Piazza Bocca della Verità].

39

TORRE DELLE MILIZIE, 13th century. The Torre delle Milizie is the most important of the many baronial towers preserved in Rome, dating from the 13th century, the time of the Comune; it stands on the slopes of the Quirinal Hill, near the Mercati Traianei (no. 5) and belonged to the Annibaldi and later the Caetani families. It is in brick, with two square blocks one above the other: the upper part with rounded corners is decorated by crenellation on the top. The tower was once very tall but was shortened in the 14th century. These fortified residences of the most powerful Roman families were a feature of the landscape of medieval Rome: the Colonna tower in Via Magnanapoli, of which little remains, and the Torre del Grillo, both 13th century; the Torre dei Conti in the Via dei Fori Imperiali, one of the most famous, destroyed in the 1348 earthquake, and the Torre degli Annibaldi in the nearby Via degli Annibaldi. [Largo Magnanapoli].

After the popes' exile in Avignon (1309-77), the city of Rome slowly began again its life as a religious capital. Renaissance architecture reached Rome late, even though since the time of Martino V Colonna (1417-71), some of the foremost Italian painters had been working for the Holy see, e.g. Gentile da Fabriano, Pisanello, Masaccio, Beato Angelico, Piero della Francesco, etc. However, the real restorer of the city was Sixtus IV della Rovere (1471-84) who undertook important projects in the fields of painting, architecture and town planning: for the decoration of the Sistine Chapel he summoned for instance Botticelli, Signorelli, Perugino, while Melozzo da Forlì carried out the frescoes in the Vatican Library. Thus Rome was launched in its new rôle as a great artistic centre where painters from different schools could meet. It was in fact during the pontificate of Sixtus' nephew, Julius II (1503-13), that Rome was to become a true artistic capital, taking over the rôle that Florence had played during the previous century. Architects working in Rome during the 16th century from Bramante onwards were building in the midst of classical monuments; they began to study these buildings, their structure and decoration, and were spurred to imitate them, even to transcend them. Thus a new style was born — that of the High Renaissance or Mannerism. Popes like Sixtus IV, Julius II, Leo X de Medici (1513-21) or Paolo III Farnese (1534-49) were real Renaissance monarchs, more interested in the political and military control of their territories than in the affairs of the church. Art, architecture, sculpture and painting were a way of glorifying the prince and his state (a similar operation was taking place in the Venetian Republic at the same period, this other great centre of Renaissance culture in Italy, not surprisingly, often in contrast with the Roman state). Cataclysmic events such as Luther's Reformation (1517) and the Sack of Rome by the Imperial troops (1527), even if they did not change papal politics, had a strong influence on contemporary art. This is the era of Mannerism, the style that began with Raffaello and achieved its greatest interpretations in the architecture of Michelangelo, Peruzzi, Vignola, and in the work of the only artist actually born in Rome, Giulio Romano (1499-1546), who, however, completed most of his work outside Rome, especially in Mantua. This style is anti-classical **par excellence**, it aims at breaking the rules of the game, it is elegant, hedonistic but also disturbing, very tense, bizarre and harrowing, «a world of disappointments, far more tragic than the Baroque world, one of struggle between spirit and matter» (Pevsner). This was to change totally with the first popes of the Counter-Reformation (1563), St. Pius V Ghisleri, and, more especially, Sixtus V Peretti (1585-90). The latter decided to make Rome the holy city, the place for pilgrimages, and for this reason redesigned the town plan to connect the great basilicas. This project changed the face of Rome and even influenced the concept of the modern city. The works of his favourite ar-

chitects (Giacomo Della Porta and Domenico Fontana) were instrumental in glorifying not a state, but the capital of reformed Catholicism. The religious dimension made itself felt once more in the world of art, and not in Rome alone.

The Early Renaissance. During the pontificate of Nicholas V (1447-55), the humanist pope who transferred the Holy See finally to the Vatican, Leon Battista Alberti worked in Rome as adviser to the Pope for the projected rebuilding of S. Pietro, as well as for the restoration of ancient monuments (S. Stefano Rotondo, no. 24) and, although no single Roman building can be attributed to him with certainty, his influence can be cleary felt in two of the great fifteenth-century buildings in Rome — Palazzo Venezia and Palazzo della Cancelleria. It was not until the pontificate of Sixtus IV della Rovere (1471-84) that the Renaissance spirit really influenced architecture in Rome. During the 14 years of this pope, architects from Tuscany, such as Bernardo Rossellino and Baccio Pontelli, and from Lombardy, Andrea Bregno, were summonned to Rome, and the first truly Renaissance churches were erected such as S. Maria del Popolo, S. Pietro in Montorio, S. Pietro in Vincoli and the Sistine Chapel itself. Sixtus also started to build the Hospital of the S. Spirito, and projected the first attempts at planning the city, he restored the Aqua Vergine conduit, extending it as far as the Fontana di Trevi, built the Ponte Sisto and made new thoroughfares — planning that was continued 20 years later under his nephew Julius II.

Melozzo da Forlì, Sixtus IV inaugurates the Vatican Library, detail of fresco (1477) in the Vatican Museum.

40

PALAZZO VENEZIA AND THE CHURCH OF S. MARCO, 1455-71. Palazzo Venezia, founded in 1455 by the Venetian Cardinal Pietro Barbo whose church of S. Marco adjoins the palazzo, is the first important Renaissance building in Rome. After Barbo had been elected pope (Paolo II, 1464-71), he chose this palazzo as his official residence, and it continued to be used by popes until the middle of the 16th century, i.e. until the Quirinal Palace had been erected (no. 62). In 1564 the palace became the Embassy of the Venetian Republic in Rome. It is half medieval stronghold, with corner tower and crenellation, and half Renaissance palazzo; the identity of the architect is uncertain, but we know that Giuliano da Sangallo was working on it from 1460. The main façade overlooking Piazza Venezia is divided by two cornices: the windows on the first floor are rectangular with marble surrounds; the elegant door is attributed to Giovanni Dalmata. The unfinished **courtyard** is surrounded by a portico with a loggia over it, reminiscent of classical models like the Colosseum: the design of the loggia has been attributed to Leon Battista Alberti. Incorporated in the palazzo is the **church of S. Marco**, founded in the 4th century and dedicated to the evangelist: it was rebuilt in the 9th century, and the mosaics in the apse date from this period. Cardinal Barbo rebuilt it yet again when the palazzo was erected in 1455, and this is the church we see today. The elegant façade in the small Piazza S. Marco has two orders, with portico and loggia formed by three arches — it was used for benedictions — repeating the motif of the adjoining courtyard; perhaps this too was the work of Alberti. It is sig-

Top left, Façade of Palazzo Venezia; top right, Façade of the church of S. Marco; above, Courtyard of Palazzo Venezia.

nificant that this first important Renaissance building in Rome is based directly on classical examples. [Piazza Venezia].

41

PALAZZO DELLA CANCELLERIA, 1485-1513. Palazzo Venezia and Palazzo della Cancelleria are the two most important early Renaissance buildings in Rome. It was begun in 1485 by Cardinal Raffaele Riario, nephew of Sixtus IV, and not finished until 1513; it housed the ecclesiastical courts (and has still extra-territorial rights). The name of the architect is not known for certain — probably it was the work of the Lombard architect Andrea Bregno with later additions by Bramante; in any case the Tuscan tradition is evident (Alberti). The beautiful wide façade in travertine is rusticated, the windows are alternated with double parastas on the upper floors, those of the first storey are decorated with the rose of the Riario family. The end bays project slightly, framing the whole building: the architecture is delicate and elegant despite the vast size of the building. The courtyard is of great interest, attributed to Bramante: of the three storeys, two lower ones with arched porticoes and on the upper floors solid walls with windows and pilasters alternating. [Corso Vittorio Emanuele].

42

PONTE SISTO, 1474. The Ponte Sisto, with its four arches, was built by Sixtus IV in 1474 in preparation for the Holy Year 1475 to replace an early Roman bridge: the architect was probably Baccio Pontelli. Halfway between the Ponte S. Angelo and the Island, it was an important link joining the two banks of the river where the city was most densely populated. It was the first of that series of urban infrastructures that pope Sixtus V was to conclude a century later (1585-90), transforming Rome into a modern city from the town-planning point of view. The two roads made by Julius II in the early 16th century on the opposite sides of the river led from the Vatican to Ponte Sisto — Via Giulia and Via della Lungara.

43

S. MARIA DEL POPOLO, 1472-77. S. Maria del Popolo, another of the buildings erected by Sixtus IV, is the most important church of the early Renaissance in Rome, where some of the best artists working in Rome in the late fifteenth and early sixteenth century — Andrea Bregno, Andrea Sansovino, Pinturicchio, Bramante, Raffaello and Sebastiano del Piombo — contributed to the construction and decoration. Originally a chapel erected in 1099 stood here, probably to celebrate the taking of Jerusalem at the end of the First Crusade. This was subsequently enlarged and then rebuilt between 1472 and 1477 on a plan attributed to Andrea Bregno, as an adjunct to the Porta Flaminia, the main entrance to the city from the north. The simple façade is divided into three, the curved cornices at the sides were added later by Bernini. Interior with three naves and side chapels, and a cupola over the presbytery — one of the first built in Rome. The **apse** was extended by **Bramante** who added a lacunar ceiling. The presbytery is decorated with beautiful frescoes by **Pinturicchio** dating from the early 16th century (the Coronation of the Virgin, Evangelists, Sybils, etc.) on the vault. They are framed by grotesque motifs, reminding us of the fashion of the period for these antique decorations. The marble altar piece designed by Andrea Bregno (1473) has been moved to the sacristy. Another early Renaissance monument is Andrea Sansovino's fine tomb of Cardinal Ascanio Sforza (died 1505), the brother of Ludovico il Moro. The **Chigi chapel**, on the left, was built by **Raffaello** not long before he died, for the Sienese banker Agostino Chigi. The artist treats the motif of the church of S. Eligio degli Orefici (no. 47) in a more elaborate way; the mosaics in the cupola were carried out from Raffaello's cartoon. The «Birth of the Virgin» by Sebastian del Piombo adorns the altar. In the left-hand transept are two masterpieces by Caravaggio, «The Conversion of St. Paul» and «The Crucifixion of St. Peter» (1601-2). [Piazza del Popolo (nos. 82 and 92)].

S. Maria del Popolo. Top left, Façade of the church; top right, Detail of frescoes by Pinturicchio, 1501; below, Medallion showing Queen Cristina of Sweden entering Rome (1655), on the right can be seen the façade of the church.

S. Maria del Popolo. Top, Bramante's apse (1507-7); immediately above, Dome of the Chigi Chapel designed by Raffaello (1516).

Top Raffaello, «The school of Athens», detail of the fresco in the Stanza della Segnatura of the Vatican (1509-10); immediately above: Palazzo Caprini, also known as the House of Raffaello, built by Bramante (1505-10) in the Borgo, and demolished in the 17th century, drawing by Palladio, 1550, (London, R.I.B.A.).

Bramante and Raffaello. Donato Bramante (1444-1514) came to Rome in 1499 when he was 55, after having worked for over 20 years at the Sforza court of Milan, where he had incorporated sumptuous decoration into clean Renaissance lines. In Rome his style underwent a complete transformation: he carried out an extremely severe interpretation of ancient architecture (the Cloister of S. Maria della Pace, the Tempietto). Julius II della Rovere (1503-13) offered Bramante the opportunity to carry out his first important large-scale project: the reconstruction of the Vatican palaces and of S. Pietro itself. Although these projects were only partially completed, they left a deep impression on the entire development of 16th century architecture. Palazzo Caprini, also known as the house of Raffaello, influenced deeply the structure of the Renaissance palace. **Raffaello** (1483-1520) came to Rome in 1509 to decorate the Vatican interiors, and must have come immediately into contact with Bramante's circle: in fact, as Peter Murray observes, «the scene painted in the fresco of the 'School of Athens' shows a building closely resembling the original project of Bramante for S. Pietro, and it is generally held that Raffaello must have been acquainted with the project». When Bramante died, Raffaello was named his successor on the project for the reconstruction of the great basilica. Raffaello's style is more elegant and daring than that of Bramante, especially in his later works, such as the Chigi chapel, Villa Madama and especially in Palazzo Branconio dell'Aquila; all these buildings herald the Mannerist style. Raffaello must also be remembered as one of the first archeologists, in the modern sense: as superintendent of Roman Antiquities, he understood the importance of surveys with maps, plans and sections of the Roman ruins so as to be able to preserve them.

44

CLOISTER OF S. MARIA DELLA PACE, Bramante, 1500-1504. The Cloister of the church of S. Maria della Pace is Bramante's first work in Rome: it was built between 1500 and 1504, and took its inspiration from that of S. Ambrogio (1490), one of his last buildings in Milan. The cloister has two storeys of nearly the same height: the arches on the ground floor have pilasters in the Roman fashion (Teatro di Marcello). The loggia with architrave on the upper storey is supported by pillars and slender columns over the centre of the arch below — giving an unusual rhythm to the cloister. The church of S. Maria della Pace built under Sixtus IV in 1482, is famous for Raffaello's fresco of the Sybils (1514), another work commissioned by the banker Agostino Chigi. The façade, with its delightful semi-circular portico, is the work of Pietro da Cortona. (no. 73). [Vicolo della Pace].

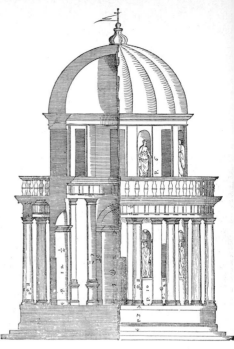

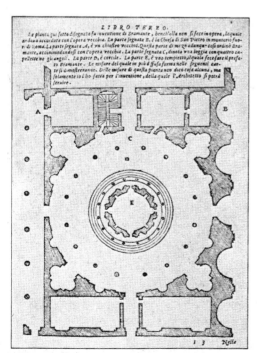

Tempietto of S. Pietro in Montorio. Top left, View of Bramante's Tempietto; top right, Section in Palladio's Quattro Libri, Venice, 1570; immediately above, Ground plan, an engraving in Serlio's Treatise, 1540.

45

TEMPIETTO OF S. PIETRO IN MONTORIO, Bramante 1502. Bramante's Tempietto, built on the spot where S. Pietro was said to have been crucified, is a version of the «martyrium» in the classical style of the High Renaissance. It is a perfect expression of the Renaissance spirit, in fact it is the only modern building illustrated by Palladio in his «Four Books of Architecture». The Tempietto was designed to stand in the centre of a circular cloister which was never built; it is a circular structure, like the Temple of Vesta (no. 10) constructed according to precise proportions. The diameter of the peristyle, 9 metres, equals the height of the cell without the cupola; there are in fact two concentric cylinders — the peristyle of Tuscan Doric columns with a high entablature (the metopes represent liturgical furnishing), crowned by a balustrade with small columns. The tambour of the cell (decorated by alternate square and shell-shaped niches) is surmounted by a perfectly hemispherical cupola; the whole building, therefore, is based on pure geometrical forms, which give it an imposing appearance, despite its modest dimensions. As Pevsner remarks: «For once, the classical Renaissance has fulfilled its declared aim of imitating classical antiquity. Here is a building which appears as nearly pure volume, as a Greek temple — beyond motifs and even beyond formal expression». The Tempietto contains the germ of future projects for S. Pietro and is the starting-point for much of future architecture, both Renaissance and Baroque. [Via Garibaldi].

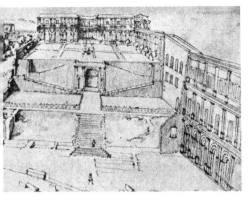

46

**THE VATICAN COURTYARDS, Bramante
1503-14.** Immediately after the election of Pope
Julius II della Rovere (1503-13), the nephew of
Sixtus IV, Bramante was commissioned to rebuild the Vatican palaces as well as S. Pietro itself — enormous projects for the architect from
Umbria: unfortunately very little remains of them.
He first designed the **Courtyard of S. Damaso**
— a series of open arches, inspired by the Colosseum, which were later closed in by glass panels,
thereby losing the original effect of light and
shade. Far more important was the **Cortile del
Belvedere** which was never completed; there
were to have been three courtyards over an area
of 300 metres, on varying levels, to link the main
buildings connecting the S. Damaso Courtyard
with the Palazzina on the Belvedere Hill, built a
decade earlier by Innocent VIII, decorated by
Mantegna. «In this work Bramante tried to imitate
both a classical amphitheatre and a classical
villa», as Murray remarks. The buildings on both
sides of the courtyard were planned with three
storeys near the Vatican Palazzo, but at the
Belvedere level they had one storey only, and the
three different levels were linked by stairs. The
courtyard ended towards the hill with a large
exedra or wide niche which masked the corner of
the earlier palazzina. The only surviving part of
this complex — apart from Bramante's general
conception — is the delightful **spiral staircase**
which is now enclosed within the Belvedere
tower. (for S. Pietro, c.f. nos. 56 and 67).

Top left, Terraced courtyard of Palazzo Belvedere in the Vatican,
in an anonymous drawing, 1540-50 (Florence, Uffizi Galleries);
top right, Detail of the Courtyard of S. Damasco; immediately
above, Spiral Staircase designed by Bramante in the Belvedere
tower.

47

S. ELIGIO DEGLI OREFICI, Raffaello, 1515.
Situated between Via Giulia and Lungotevere, the small church of S. Eligio degli Orefici was Raffaello's first attempt at architecture. It has a Greek cross plan, surmounted by a hemispheric cupola above a high tambour: its lines are crystalline in their purity, as, indeed, is the rest of this building in which grey pillars against white walls give the whole interior a severe elegance. It is one of the most harmonious constructions of the Roman Renaissance, worthy to be the church of the goldsmiths' guild. In the **Chigi Chapel** in S. Maria del Popolo (no. 43), a later project of Raffaello's, the artist shows off his ability of decorating in the most magnificent high Renaissance style. The church of S. Eligio was completed after Raffaello's death by Baldassare Peruzzi: the façade is the work of Flaminio Ponzio (1602). [Via S. Eligio].

48

VILLA MADAMA, Raffaello 1516-17. Raffaello began building Villa Madama on the slopes of Monte Mario in 1515 for Cardinal Giuliano de' Medici, the future Pope Clement VII; it susequently became the property of Margherita of Parma, daughter of Charles V (she is the «Madama»). It is now the property of the Foreign Ministry. The villa was never completed and is only a small part of the grandiose original project which was to have included a circular courtyard, residential and ceremonial buildings, stables, terraces and gardens on various levels, as well as the cavea of an open-air theatre built into the hillside. With his project, Raffaello evidently wanted to imitate the Roman monuments, such as baths and imperial palaces not only as regards structure but also wall decoration as well. In fact this is the first example of a new genre of building, the great Renaissance villa. The windows of the exedra in front of the entrance (part of the circular courtyard) are framed by brick columns: this fashion for «unfinished surfaces» was inspired by the Roman ruins and heralds Mannerism. The wide loggia with its three bays and central cupola has a niche at one end with a half-cupola, entirely decorated by elegant stucco-work and frescoes by Giovanni da Udine and Giulio Romano, in direct imitation of those in the Domus Aurea (no. 7) which had recently been discovered and excavated, revealing its «grotesque» decoration. [Via di Villa Madama].

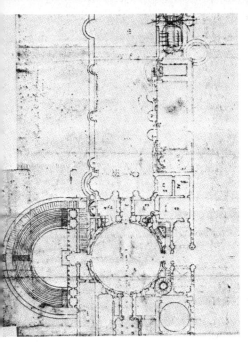

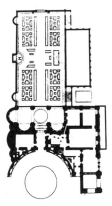

49

PALAZZO VIDONI CAFFARELLI, Raffaello, c. 1515. This Palazzo, attributed to Raffaello, is one of the most interesting Renaissance constructions in Rome. Despite alterations (a top floor was added later) and having been subsequently enlarged, it still preserves intact the original façade overlooking Via del Sudario. The façade repeats the theme Bramante used in Palazzo Caprini, but Raffaello's interpretation is entirely original. This is a residential building above a row of shops (the Roman «insula»); the ground floor has long strips of smooth rusticated stone forming an elegant ornamental motif, whereas the upper floor emphasises the vertical theme with tall, narrow windows with architraves and twin Doric half-columns. The courtyard is severe but graceful. [Via del Sudario].

Opposite page: top right, Exedra of Villa Madama; this page, top, Plan of the Villa by Sangallo the Younger from Raffaello, c. 1520 (Florence, Uffizi); immediately above, Plan of the Villa.

50

PALAZZO SPADA, Merisi, c. 1540. Palazzo Spada, near Piazza Farnese, was built around 1540 by Giulio Merisi da Caravaggio for Cardinal Capo di Ferro, later sold to Cardinal Spada (now the seat of the Consiglio di Stato) and is one of the most magnificent 16th century palaces in Rome. It reminds us of Palazzo Branconio dell'Aquila, one of Raffaello's last works and clearly Mannerist in style (this building was demolished in the 17th century for the construction of the new Piazza S. Pietro). The façade of Palazzo Spada is decorated with stucco work by Giulio Mazzoni (1556-60); the ground floor is smoothly rusticated, while the first floor windows alternate with niches containing statues of famous figures of antiquity. The mezzanine floor has small square windows decorated with garlands and medallions: the top floor windows alternate with inscriptions referring to the figures on the first floor. The stuccoes in the courtyard are even more elaborate. In 1635 Borromini made some alterations, adding the garden wall and the famous colonnade with its trompe l'oeil perspective in the garden gallery; it seems it inspired Bernini's Scala Regia in the Vatican (no. 67). [Piazza Capo di Ferro].

Peruzzi and Michelangelo. Baldassare Peruzzi (1481-1536), painter, architect and stage designer worked in Siena under the influence of Pinturicchio and Francesco di Giorgio Martini: he went to Rome when he was 20, associating with Bramante and then Raffaello. After the death of Raffaello, he was appointed architect of S. Pietro with Antonio da Sangallo the Younger; he also completed Raffaello's church of S. Eligio degli Orefici. With Sangallo he designed Villa Farnese at Caprarola. Villa Farnesina and Palazzo Massimo alle Colonne are considered to be his masterpieces: in them Peruzzi shows a capacity for originality and an elegance (which Pevsner describes as) «an almost feminine delicacy» which make this artist one of the first and most distinguished exponents of Mannerism in architecture. He was a skilled draughtsman and many of his projects were published by Serlio in his Trattato (1537) which was circulated all over Europe, influencing many architects (the first oval-shaped buildings). Completely different in character was **Antonio da Sangallo the Younger** (1483-1546): he came to Rome from Florence in 1505 with his uncle Giuliano, to continue the family tradition of expert builders. Like his contemporary, Peruzzi, he worked with Bramante and Raffaello but was more of an engineer than an architect (Bastions of the Aurelian Walls, no. 1), part of the 15th century tradition, he is famous as the architect of Palazzo Farnese. **Michelangelo Buonarroti** (1475-1564) met with great success in Rome both as a sculptor (tomb of Julius II, 1505) and as a painter (ceiling of the Sistine Chapel, 1508, Last Judgement, 1536) under Pope Julius II, but only much later was he given the opportunity to design great architectural projects, although he had already built the Medici Chapel and the Laurenziana Library in Florence during the 1420s. When he undertook the plans for the Campidoglio and the Basilica of S. Pietro, he was over 70. From 1560 he worked on projects for Porta Pia (no. 1), the church of S. Maria degli Angeli in Diocletian's Baths (no. 21) and the Sforza Chapel in S. Maria Maggiore (no. 25) — all of which were completed after his death. He approached architecture from a sculptor's point of view, rejecting classical rules to bring his constructions to life with the most original plastic forms, creating a sense of tension and restlessness typical of the Mannerist period. His influence was to make itself felt particularly in the following century.

51

FARNESINA, Baldassare Peruzzi, 1508-11.
The Villa Farnesina is Peruzzi's first work in
Rome, built between 1508-1511 for the Sienese
banker Agostino Chigi, protector of Peruzzi who
also came from Siena. It was a suburban villa set
amidst gardens beside the Tiber in Via della Lungara which Julius II had made; it was later bought
by the Farnese family and treated almost as
though it were an extension on the opposite side
of the river of the great palace begun by Antonio
da Sangallo the Younger in 1514 (no. 53). At present it houses the Gabinetto Nazionale delle
Stampe (a collection of prints). The Farnesina is
therefore one of the earliest and most imitated
examples of the Renaissance villa: it was designed for ceremonial occasions, for relaxation,
receptions and parties. This is a delightfully elegant building both as regards the architecture and
the decoration of the interiors carried out by
Peruzzi himself, as well as by Raffaello, Sebastiano del Piombo, Giulio Romano and Sodoma.
The main façade is harmoniously simple: two
storeys with windows framed by light pilasters,
while along the level of the attic windows, under
the cornice, there is a sumptuous sculptured
frieze with cherubs and garlands. On the side
overlooking the garden, the building is U-shaped
with two projecting wings framing the ground-
floor loggia which was to be decorated by Raffaello and his school (1517), transforming it into
an open-air pergola with the stories of Psyche;
the architecture, the decoration and the garden
setting combine to achieve perfection. Peruzzi's

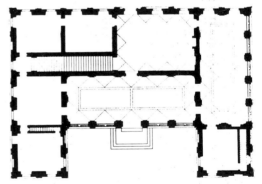

The Farnesina. Top left, façade overlooking the garden; top
right, Peruzzi, trompe l'oeil perspective in the Hall of the Columns, 1517-18; immediately above, Ground plan of the Villa.

fresco in the main room is one of the earliest Renaissance examples of «trompe l'oeil», depicting
a view of Rome. [Via della Lungara].

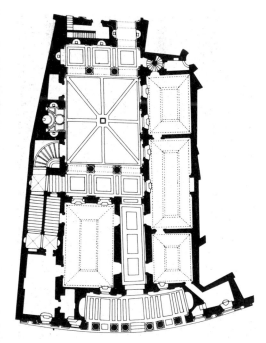

52

PALAZZO MASSIMO ALLE COLONNE, Baldassare Peruzzi, 1532-36. Palazzo Massimo, known as «alle Colonne», was built by Baldassare Peruzzi between 1532-36 for the brothers Pietro and Angelo Massimo on the site of an earlier palace belonging to the Massimo family which had been destroyed during the Sack of Rome (1527). The new palazzo stands on the old Via Papale (now Corso Vittorio Emanuele) and has a curved façade (the earlier building stood on the foundations of an old Roman theatre dating from the time of Diocletian) and has a completely original design. The ground floor with its sturdy portico of six columns is quite separate from the upper storeys; the windows are not alternated with pilasters or columns and are simply designed on the smooth rustication of the wall with no cornices, giving a feeling of fluidity to the curved façade. The mezzanine windows are small and square; those above the first floor have their frames decorated with ribbon moulding — much imitated subsequently particularly in northern Europe. The courtyard is equally original: over the architrave of the portico are unadorned oblong apertures without frames which are part of the portico, to reduce the height, making it resemble that of the loggia above, giving better proportions and a feeling of lightness to the courtyard. This is original, elegant architecture, studied in all its details, one of the most successful inventions of early Roman Mannerism. [Corso Vittorio Emanuele].

Palazzo Massimo alle Colonne. Top left, Façade; top right, Detail of the Courtyard; immediately above, Ground plan of the palazzo (Letaronilly).

53

PALAZZO FARNESE, Antonio da Sangallo the Younger, 1534-80. Palazzo Farnese forms one whole side of Piazza Farnese, and stretches back to the Via Giulla, almost to the Tiber: it is the most magnificent of 16th century palaces in Rome. It was originally commissioned by Cardinal Alessadro Farnese in 1514; the architect was Antonio da Sangallo the Younger. When Farnese became pope, Paul III (1534-49), the building was enlarged and altered - this is the palazzo we see today. When Sangallo died in 1546, Michelangelo continued the work which was completed by Giacomo della Porta in 1589 (the façade overlooking the garden). It is now the seat of the French Embassy. It is a vast construction, an isolated square block: the façade in the Piazza has three floors separated by long cornices; the style is somewhat academic, harking back to the 15th century Tuscan tradition. The heavy cornice above the second storey and the central balcony over the entrance were added by Michelangelo. The imposing entrance is formed by a carriageway with a barrel-vaulted roof, separated from the side pavements by red grannite columns; the courtyard is in the style of Bramante and has three orders of arcades (Colosseum) which were probably walled up subsequently on the two upper storeys. The top floor is clearly the work of a different hand — that of Michelangelo. The interior is richly decorated, particularly the gallery with its frescoes by Annibale Carracci (1597-1604). [Piazza Farnese].

Palazzo Farnese. Top, Façade overlooking Piazza Farnese; immediately above, Carriage entrance with side pavements.

54

PIAZZA DEL CAMPIDOGLIO, Michelangelo / Giacomo della Porta, 1536-1605. The Piazza del Campidoglio, designed by Michelangelo, was commissioned by Paolo III Farnese in 1536: the buildings were begun 10 years later. The Capitoline Hill had been the centre of the civic administration of Rome since early times: during the Middle Ages it was an open space dominated by a fortified construction above the tabularium, the Palazzo Senatorio. In 1538 when the Piazza was redesigned, the equestrian statue of Marcus Aurelius (no. 9) was taken from beside the old Lateran Palace and placed in the centre of the Campidoglio; it is said that the statue escaped destruction because the rider was thought to have been Constantine. The rebuilding proceeded so slowly that Michelangelo managed to complete only the splendid double flight of steps of the Palazzo Senatorio, while the rest of this building and the two side palaces, Palazzo dei Conservatori and that of the Capitoline Museum, were all built by Giacomo della Porta from 1563 and completed only in the 17th century; he exe-cuted Michelangelo's original plans quite closely, however. The Piazza del Campidoglio was the first of the great squares of Rome to be planned in the modern era: it is shaped like a trapezium, with the central element, the statue of Marcus Aurelius, emphasised by the elegant oval markings on the pavement. One reaches the Piazza by climbing a long ramp of steps: at the top are two marble statues of Dioscuri, sculptures of the Imperial Roman epoch, decorating the balustrade. At the far end stands the Palazzo Senatorio, the Town Hall of Rome; it is composed of two storeys above a high footing, united by giant pilasters. This motif of giant pillars linking two storeys (used here for the first time) is repeated on the side buildings, giving the Piazza an element of unity. All three palazzi are crowned by balustrades decorated by statues, similar to the Marciana Library in Venice, built by Jacopo Sansovino in 1537 to complete the Piazzetta S. Marco, the Venetian Campidoglio. [Piazza del Campidoglio].

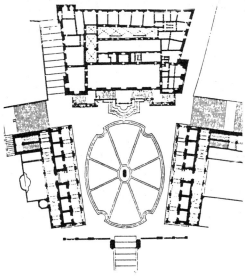

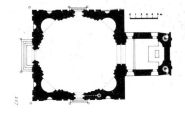

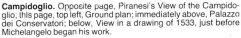

Campidoglio. Opposite page, Piranesi's View of the Campidoglio, this page, top left, Ground plan; immediately above, Palazzo dei Conservatori; below, View in a drawing of 1533, just before Michelangelo began his work.

55

S. MARIA DI LORETO, Antonio da Sangallo the Younger, 1510-85. The church of S. Maria di Loreto near Trajan's forum was built around 1510 by Antonio da Sangallo the Younger who had recently come to Rome with his uncle, Giuliano. It is a small structure, a cube outside and inside an octagon, inspired by the halls in the Roman baths. The façades are divided into three by twin pilasters on an uninterrupted base: clean, simple lines, Tuscan rather than in the Bramante tradition. The tambour and cupola were added later by Jacopo del Duca (1577-85). This church, the 18th-century SS. Nome di Maria by Dériset (1736) and Trajan's column (no. 5) close by, form one of the most scenic groups of monuments in the centre of Rome, here the city seems to be a palimpsest, one period superimposed upon another over the centuries. [Fori Imperiali].

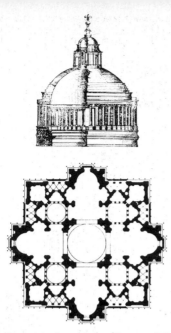

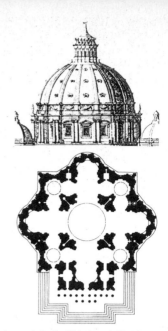

Project for the dome and ground plan of Bramante (1506).

Dome and ground plan by Michelangelo (1547).

56

ST. PETER'S IN THE VATICAN, Michelangelo / Della Porta, 1547-90. Under Constantine (319-50), the basilica of S. Pietro was an enormous church with a Latin cross plan, five naves and an imposing courtyard in front. In 1452, Niccolò V decided to rebuild the 1000-year old basilica with advice from Alberti, and commissioned Bernardo Rossellino to build a new apse. The idea of a totally new church was revived by Julius II who commissioned Bramante with the immense task, to be helped by Fra Giocondo and Giuliano da Sangallo. Bramante decided on a Greek cross plan with a hemispherical cupola above — i.e. he wanted to raise the Pantheon over Constantine's old basilica, harking back to the form of the martyrium as he had done in his Tempietto di S. Pietro in Montorio (no. 45). Work began in 1506 and was interrupted in 1514 by the death of Bramante when the piers and arches to support the cupola had been constructed. Raffaello succeeded Bramante, to be followed by Peruzzi and Antonio da Sangallo the Younger: they proposed various solutions but the work did not proceed. 30 years later, in 1547, Paolo III Farnese commissioned Michelangelo who almost completed the project. He went back to Bramante's idea of the Greek cross with the cupola «but where Bramante had intended sub-centres repeating on a smaller scale the motif of the main centre, Michelangelo cut off the arms of the sub-centres, thus condensing the composition into one central dome resting on piers. Bramante would have re-futed this as colossal, i.e. inhuman, and on a square peripheral ambulatory» (Pevsner). The exterior — apses, ends of the transepts — is composed of a series of gigantic Corinthian pillars in pairs which emphasise the verticality of the construction, supporting a robust attic storey which repeats the motifs below. The tambour of the dome consists of a series of twin columns alternating with large windows. In place of Bramante's smooth hemispherical cupola, Michelangelo designed an ogival one similar to Brunelleschi's in Florence, but with double ribs to emphasise the sturdy nature of the construction. This cupola is 136.5 metres high, its diameter is 42 metres, slightly less than that of the Pantheon. Michelangelo died in 1564 without seeing his work completed: the building, including that of the great dome and smaller cupolas, was finished by Giacomo della Porta about 1590, according to Michelangelo's plans. The latter had designed a façade with a double portico consisting of a row of 10 columns and 4 more in the centre. The façade we see today and the eastern end is the work of Carlo Maderno (no. 67), who transformed S. Pietro into a church with a Latin cross plan. The concept of both Bramante and Michelangelo of a central plan dominated by a great dome can now be appreciated only from the apse and the side transepts: notwithstanding these changes, S. Pietro today is still Michelangelo's greatest work of architecture in Rome. [Piazza S. Pietro].

Michelangelo. Above, Apse and dome of S. Pietro; below, Detail of frescoes in the Sistine Chapel (1508) by Michelangelo.

Vignola and the late sixteenth century.
Jacopo Barozzi, known as **Vignola** (1507-73), a painter and architect from Emilia who had worked in Bologna, a follower of Serlio whom he had met in France, was the most important architect working in Rome during the second half of the 16th century: he came to Rome in the 1550s and was protected by the Farnese family. He completed the Villa at Caprarola which Peruzzi had begun, and worked on the family palazzo in Piacenza. His masterpiece is Villa Giulia, an open structure, with free-flowing space typical of the Mannerist period. An innovator in the field of religious architecture (S. Andrea in Via Flaminia, S. Anna dei Palafrenieri), he built the church which set a new fashion in the history of Counter-Reformation architecture — the Gesù. His treatise on the orders of architecture was received all over Europe with great success. **Pirro Ligorio** (1510-83), a Neapolitan painter and architect, an expert in antiquities, was the last important figure in the history of Roman Mannerism: he planned one of the most famous «Italian» gardens — that of Villa d'Este at Tivoli, as well as the Casina of Pius IV in the Vatican where he also built the niche of the Belvedere. Pope Pius IV Medici (1559-65) was the last 16th-century pope to have princely ambitions in the field of architecture, he also commissioned Michelangelo to build the church of S. Maria degli Angeli and Porta Pia. Under S. Pius V Ghisleri (1566-72), the Dominican pope, friend of Carlo Borromeo, the Catholic restoration of the Counter-Reformation began; the Council of Trent, concluded in 1563, imposed new rules in the field of art. One of the best architects of this period is the Genoese **Giacomo della Porta** (1533-1602), a disciple of Michelangelo and Vignola, he completed several buildings begun by his masters — the Campidoglio, Palazzo Farnese, S. Pietro (he built the dome — his masterpiece), the façade and cupola of the Gesù, as well as working on many other churches (e.g. S. Luigi dei Francesi, S. Atanasio dei Greci, S. Andrea della Valle) and palazzi, e.g. the Sapienza, the Collegio Clementino, Palazzo Aldobrandini and the same family's villa at Frascati, and some fountains. Della Porta probably built more in Rome than any other architect has done, giving the city that severe character typical of the architecture of the last decades of the century, before the Baroque explosion. Finally **Domenico Fontana** should be mentioned (1543-1607), the founder of a family of architects which had moved to Rome from Ticino: he was the adviser of Sixtus V Peretti (1585-90) in the new town-planning of the city of straight roads all converging on one point, still in existence today.

57
CASINA OF POPE PIUS IV, Ligorio, 1558-61.
Pope Pius IV's Casina in the Vatican gardens is one of the most elegant, scenic buildings in the Mannerist style in Rome, the masterpiece of Pirro Ligorio (1558-61) who here gives us proof of his ability as a stage designer and garden architect (Villa d'Este at Tivoli). On either side of a terrace in the form of an oval courtyard stand two buildings: the larger one has a façade covered with highly ornate stucco work, the smaller has a portico and an attic, crowned by a tympanum. On the ground floor there is a nympheum with fountains and statues. [Vatican Gardens].

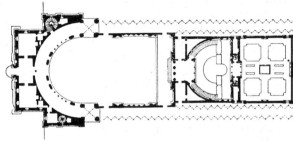

Villa Giulia. Above, Façade overlooking the courtyard; right, Ground plan; below, right, Detail of the loggia of the nymphaeum.

58

VILLA GIULIA, Vignola / Ammannati, 1552-53.
Villa Giulia was built in 1552-53 for Pope Julius III by several architects: the main work was done by Vignola and Ammannati with contributions from Vasari and Michelangelo. The villa was inspired by Villa Madama (no. 48) and by Pliny's descriptions of the **villa suburbana**. Today it houses the Etruscan Museum (Museo Nazionale di Villa Giulia). The main building consists of a simply designed façade with a central entrance in the form of a triumphal arch. On the other side the building forms a semi-circle overlooking the first courtyard, at the end of which is a loggia giving onto the nympheum, and beyond that another loggia overlooking the garden. It is a succession of straight and curved lines with open spaces typical of Mannerist architecture. In the garden on the right stands a 19th-century reconstruction of a small Etruscan-Italian temple. [Viale delle Belle Arti].

59

VILLA MEDICI, A. Lippi, 1564. Villa Medici was built for Cardinal Giovanni Ricci in 1564 by Annibale Lippi; later it was acquired by the Medici family; since 1803 it has been the Roman premises of the French Academy, founded by Louis XIV in 1666. The front façade is fairly simple but the side facing the garden is most original in conception: there are two projecting side wings, which are lower than the central block, and are surmounted by towers. The central part, on two storeys, has a large portico on the ground floor. The walls are covered with stucco ornaments as well as fragments of antique bas-reliefs (some taken from the Ara Pacis, no. 9). [Viale della Trinità dei Monti].

60

S. ANDREA DI VIA FLAMINIA, Vignola, 1554. This small church is the first religious building of Vignola, completed in 1554 for Julius III, the pope who had recently commissioned him to design the famous Villa Giulia (no. 58). S. Andrea, although minute, is a most interesting construction, it consists of a cube covered by an oval cupola — something that had not been seen before. In 1572, Vignola planned another small church, S. Anna dei Palafrenieri in Vaticano: this time the ground plan is oval — a feature later much used in Baroque architecture, that probably has its origin in studies made by Peruzzi (such as those for S. Domenico in Siena). It should be remembered that in 1552 Jacopo Sansovino built the church of the Ospedale degli Incurabili in Venice (demolished in the 19th century) also with an oval ground plan. [Via Flaminia].

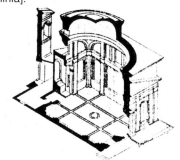

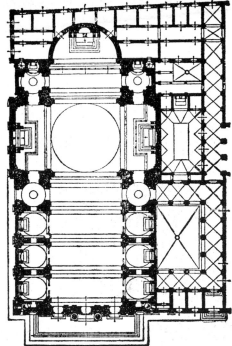

61

CHURCH OF THE GESÙ, Vignola 1568-75.

The church of the Gesù was begun by Vignola in 1568 for the Jesuit order: it was the first church to be built for this religious order and was to have an enormous influence on all subsequent religious architecture. The building had to meet particular specifications: it had to accommodate a large congregation and enable them all to hear the sermons, a fundamental aspect of the new Counter-Reformation liturgy — hence the wide nave and barrel vaulting for good acoustics. The Latin cross plan meets these needs admirably: there are no side naves, only a series of chapels along the side walls, a plan probably derived from Alberti's church of S. Andrea in Mantua (1470); the transept of the Gesù, however is much shorter, creating more space under the cupola and throwing more light on the high altar and the side altars dedicated to S. Ignatius and S. Francis Xavier, the first Jesuit saints. The interior was renewed in the late 17th century — originally it was far more severe. The façade is not as Vignola designed it: it was built after his death in 1573 by Giacomo della Porta who gave less emphasis to the central block. Not far from this church is the enormous building of the **Collegio Romano**, the Jesuit school: another typical Counter-Reformation building attributed to Bartolomeo Ammannati and characterised by a purity of line that is almost Neo-Classical. (1582-84). [Piazza del Gesù].

Church del Gesù. Top left, Façade; top right, Plan; immediately above, Façade of the Collegio Romano, Ammannati, 1582.

62

PALAZZO AND PIAZZA DEL QUIRINALE

Mascherino / Fontana, 1572-90. The Quirinal Palace was the largest building constructed by the Renaissance popes outside the Vatican, and substituted Palazzo Venezia as their city residence. A large area of land had to be acquired for its construction, previously occupied by villas and gardens of rich families such as the Farnese, Colonna, Carpi and Grimani; it necessitated the demolition of the vast Baths of Constantine where the famous horses stood who gave the Piazza its former name — Monte Cavallo. Already during the 1550s Paul IV wanted to buy the Farnese gardens to build his summer residence; then Gregory XIII commissioned Martino Longhi the Elder to design a palazzo in 1572. The building was restructured by the same pope: the new project was by Ottavio Mascherino. From this time the Quirinal Palace became the «secular headquarters» of the pope and was to remain so for 300 years until the unification of Italy, when it became the official residence of the Head of the Italian State. It is a sumptuous palace combining the functional character of a town residence with the advantages of a country house, set in an enormous garden stretching over most of the Quirinal Hill. The actual palazzo is not particularly distinguished from an architectural point of view, even though many architects had a hand in its design in the late 16th and early 17th centuries: Mascherino, Domenico Fontana (the courtyard), Flaminio Ponzio and Carlo Maderno who designed the entrance from the piazza, decorated with statues of St. Peter and St. Paul. Domenico Fontana laid out the piazza with the statues of the Dioscuri and the fountain. Under Urban VIII, in the early 17th century, the large garden was laid out, one of the most important of the Baroque period, necessitating the final demolition of Constantine's Baths, levelling of the hilly terrain and the construction of garden walls. [Piazza del Quirinale].

Quirinale. Top, Façade and Via Pia (now via del Quirinale and via XX Settembre) from Piranesi's engraving; immediately above, Spiral staircase designed by Mascherino.

63

PALAZZO LATERANO, Fontana, 1586. The Lateran Palace had been the papal residence from the time of Constantine (c.f. nos. 23, 35) up to the return of the pope from Avignon: by then the original buildings had been destroyed by fire; later the Holy See was transferred to the Vatican. Sixtus V decided to rebuild the palace in 1586 as part of his great project of revitalising the old basilicas: the commission was given to Domenico Fontana. This is the period when new roads were made, transforming the medieval aspect of the city, with obelisks at road junctions; the obelisk of Piazza San Giovanni in Laterano had been brought to Rome from Thebes (15th century B.C.) by Constantine II to stand at the centre of the Circus Maximus. The equestrian statue of Marcus Aurelius once stood in the Lateran square: it is now in the Piazza del Campidoglio (no. 54). Fontana's palace seems to be a subdued version of Palazzo Farnese (no. 53), interpreting the Counter-Reformation spirit of austerity, imposed by Sixtus V at the close of the century, which was also applied to contemporary architecture.

In 1646, Innocent X Pamphili commissioned Borromini to restore the old **basilica** but without altering the original structure. Borromini could not rebuild it, but the additions he made are significant. In the interior, he alternated niches and arches between gigantic pilasters: the ornate 16th-century ceiling was left. Borromini exploited the varying heights of the ceilings in the side naves with great originality. One century later, Alessandro Galilei completed the majestic **façade** (1735) in a style which heralds the new Neo-classical fashion.

[Piazza S. Giovanni in Laterano].

Top left, Façade of the Palazzo Laterano; top right, Façade of the Basilica of S. Giovanni Laterano (Galilei, 1735); Detail of the side nave of the basilica, restored by Borromini, 1646.

Following the initial dismay at the Lutheran revolution, the Roman Catholic church reacted with the Counter-Reformation and felt itself increasingly strong and ultimately triumphant, supported wholeheartedly as it was by the countries who were still Catholic. The construction of monumental works and the renewed patronage of the arts thus became one of the main manifestations of the revived prestige of the Catholic capital which seemed to be imitating the pomp of the great absolute monarchies. The Counter-Reformation ideology, for that matter, considered the visual arts to be an efficacious instrument for religious propaganda, and as a means of involving the faithful emotionally in the acceptance of the new rigid principles, particularly by the action of religious orders such as the Jesuits, the Theatines, the Barnabites, etc. who were gradually becoming more powerful in all the Catholic countries. Baroque art is, therefore, on the one hand, intensely religious (Bernini, for example, was a committed Catholic) and on the other hand it could be pure conformity; it is also frankly sumptuous, inventive, and, in a sense, giving scope to new energies. Particularly in the period 1620-60, Rome began to change its appearance in a spectacular way, acquiring that Baroque aspect which still characterises it today: this was largely due to the initiatives of popes such as Urban VIII Barberini (1623-44), another Julius II, who employed Bernini on St. Peter's and Palazzo Barberini; Innocent X Pamphili (1644-55), responsible for Piazza Navona, the restoration of the Lateran basilica; Alexander VII Chigi (1655-67) who laid out St. Peter's Square and Piazza del Popolo. The architects mainly responsible for all this rebuilding were Bernini and Borromini whose art work lies at the very roots of subsequent European Baroque. Bernini's Baroque is classical, as is that of Pietro da Cortona, the architectural equivalent of Poussin's painting: it had parallels in the dignified, disciplined work of Longhena in Venice, of Mansart in France or of Wren in England, i.e. in those countries that were less involved with the Counter-Reformation, or which actually rejected it; a century later this Baroque developed into the rationalist purism of neo-Classicism. The visionary art of Borromini, comparable only to the work of El Greco or Caravaggio in painting, and of Mochi, the anti-Bernini, in sculpture, was to have most success in Piedmont and in southern Italy; abroad Borromini provided inspiration for the Rococò style in Austria, southern Germany and Spain — all Counter-Reformation countries, and ones in which the late Gothic tradition had continued.

Maderno and Bernini. During the papacy of Paul V Borghese (1605-21) the climate of the artistic world began to change, even if there were few changes in the field of religion. Work on the completion of St. Peter's was resumed by Maderno, while the papal residence on the Quirinal and the Cappella Paolina in S. Maria Maggiore (no. 25) were decorated with unprecedented magnificence; during the same period, cardinal Scipione Borghese, a nephew of the pope, began his rôle as a great patron of the arts. The favourite architect of the Borghese family, **Flaminio Ponzio** (1560-1613), from Varese, was still designing buildings in the late Mannerist style. Maderno, on the other hand, was an innovator. **Carlo Maderno** (1556-1629) came from Lake Lugano as did his uncle Domenico Fontana who summoned him to Rome to collaborate with him. In 1603 he carried out his first independent work, the façade of the church of S. Susanna, and in the same year he was nominated director of the works in the basilica of St. Peter's; Maderno was also responsible for the elegant cupola of S. Andrea della Valle and the original project for Palazzo Barberini. In these buildings Maderno developed a strong, severe style which influenced much contemporary architecture, in particular the early works of the greatest Baroque architects, Bernini and Borromini.

Gian Lorenzo Bernini (1598-1680) was born in Naples and soon went to Rome to work with his father, a well-known sculptor. Bernini had a long, successful career as sculptor, painter, architect, town-planner and stage designer. He is comparable only to Michelangelo as regards his many-sided genius and the enormous influence he had in all fields of art. His architecture, like that of Michelangelo, possesses a structural clarity and precision of detail which give his buildings a sculptural quality, even though we can always feel his classical background — he was, in fact, a great admirer of artists such as Palladio and Poussin. In his buildings, Bernini often skilfully introduces elements of sculpture, painting and stucco decoration, as for example, in the Cornaro Chapel in S. Maria della Vittoria, perhaps his most famous work — and the most essentially Baroque — on account of its expressive intensity. During his long career he worked mostly as a sculptor: his architectural works are comparatively few — four churches, (S. Bibiana, S. Andrea al Quirinale, churches at Castelgandolfo and Ariccia), three palaces (Barberini — which Maderno had begun — Montecitorio — which he left unfinished — and Palazzo Chigi which was subsequently altered), and his work on St. Peter's in the Vatican, including his great project for St. Peter's Square. His fame was such that Luigi XIV, king of France, asked his advice about rebuilding the Louvre.

64

PALAZZO BORGHESE, Ponzio / Vasanzio, 1605-15. The papacy of Paul V Borghese was a transitional period between the early Counter-Reformation and the splendours of the Baroque; during this period, patronage of the arts became fashionable once more, thanks to the enthusiasm and the taste of Cardinal Scipione Borghese, the pope's nephew, who succeeded in forming an extraordinary collection of works of art by old masters such as Raffaello, Tiziano, Veronese, etc., and also works of contemporary artists such as Caravaggio, Guido Reni, Bernini, etc. Cardinal Borghese completed the family residence and constructed the Casino in the gardens of Villa Borghese, employing Flaminio Ponzio and later Giovanni Vasanzio as architects.
Palazzo Borghese (1605-14), occupying an irregularly-shaped site, has one façade designed by Ponzio in the tradition of Palazzo Farnese, while the scenic courtyard with its double colonnade was a novelty in Rome (the idea probably came from northern Italy - Genoa); it overlooks a splendid garden with a lily pond - one of the best preserved of this period, designed by Carlo Rainaldi in 1670. The **Casino di Villa Borghese** (1613-15) in the Pincio (it now houses the Borghese Gallery and Museum), designed by Vasanzio, is a country house surrounded by gardens: it takes its inspiration from the Villa Farnesina (no. 51) and from Villa Medici (no. 59) especially as regards the richly decorated façade. In this way, what might be called the second Roman Renaissance, the Baroque style, was launched.
[Piazza Borghese / Villa Borghese].

65

S. SUSANNA, façade, Maderno 1603. In 1603 Carlo Maderno completed the façade of the church of S. Susanna, a very early church which had been rebuilt in 1475. This is a strong, clear structure, Maderno's masterpiece, which marked the beginning of a new era in the history of Roman architecture, rather like the innovations of Annibale Carracci and Caravaggio in the field of painting. The structure of the façade resembles that of the Gesù church (no. 61), but the decoration is more concentrated towards the centre and bolder in conception; the intervals between columns «increase towards the centre, and the wall surface is gradually eclipsed by Mannerist scrolls, niches with figures and the entrance which occupies the central space between the columns» (Wittkower). It should be noted that at this intersection of Via XX Settembre there are two other important churches dating from the same period: **S. Bernardo alle Terme**, built in one of the corner rotondas of the Baths of Diocletian (no. 21), which contains an interesting group of sculptures by Camillo Mariani (c. 1600), and **S. Maria della Vittoria**, also by Maderno, but completed after his death, in which is the famous **Cappella Cornaro**, decorated by what is perhaps Bernini's greatest work - the group showing S. Teresa transfixed by the love of God (1646).
[Via XX Settembre].

66

PALAZZO BARBERINI, Maderno / Bernini, 1628-33. In 1628 Pope Urban VIII Barberini (1623-44) commissioned Maderno to design a family residence in Via delle Quattro Fontane. Maderno, whose assistant was Borromini, died the following year and the work was continued by Bernini who completed the palazzo in 1633, again with the help of Borromini. For this reason it is difficult to attribute the various features of the building to any one of the three architects. The building, a country residence, has an H-shaped plan, a courtyard in front of the façade, with two projecting wings, like the Farnesina (no. 51). The façade consists of three stories with an open portico on the ground floor: the windows on the top storey are framed by a curious trompe l'oeil perspective. The richly decorated windows between the façade and the wings are certainly the work of Borromini. The oval staircase on the right of the portico is probably also by Borromini, whereas the rectangular one on the left is thought to be the work of Bernini. This palazzo, one of the most magnificent in 17th century Rome (it now houses the Rome National Gallery), is decorated with frescoes by Pietro da Cortona (1633-39). [Via delle Quattro Fontane].

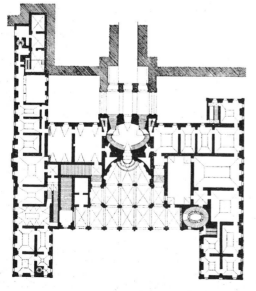

Above, Piazza S. Pietro; right, Engraving by Falda (1676) showing Bernini's project for the third central colonnade which was never built.

67

ST. PETER'S IN THE VATICAN, façade and nave, Maderno, 1605-14; interior and Piazza S. Pietro, Bernini, 1624-68. After the building of Michelangelo's basilica (no. 56) had been completed, there was an interval and debate about enlarging the structure in the light of the new needs of the Counter-Reformation. In 1605, Paul V finally commissioned Carlo Maderno to lengthen the nave to alter Michelangelo's Greek cross plan into a Latin cross: thus three bays and the portico were added. Then Maderno designed the façade which was completed in 1614. These alterations, unfortunately, interfere with Michelangelo's original concept, in which the huge dome dominated the Greek cross plan: with the new façade, the dome is now hidden. In his design for the **façade**, Maderno attempted to follow the original designs of Michelangelo, using giant Corinthian columns and pilasters. The two side bays on which two bell towers were to have been raised (but were never built) are later additions. In 1629, Bernini was appointed architect of the basilica: five years previously he had already begun the construction of the baldacchino; in fact he continued working on the basilica, and on the Piazza in front of the church, for the rest of his life.

He worked not only as architect and sculptor, but also as town-planner and, it might be said, as stage designer - that fusion of all the arts so typical of the Baroque style. The **Baldacchino** placed over the tomb of S. Pietro (1624-33) was the first of Bernini's commitments, and one of the most difficult: a work in which architecture and sculpture are perfectly integrated on a gigantic scale (it is 29 metres high), but in proportion with the enormous space of the dome directly above it. The four twisted bronze columns (the same form as those of the original ciborium) contrasting with the white marble of the interior, support «hangings» in bronze, an imitation of the traditional baldacchino used by the pope during processions (there is no trabeation): at the top of the columns stand four bronze angels with the four volutes supporting a golden globe, surmounted by a cross. From the central nave, the canopy frames another spectacular work by Bernini, in gilded bronze, the Throne of St. Peter, (1656-66) in the apse, representing the origins of papal power, surmounted by saints and angels and the Holy Spirit in the form of a dove. In these two works, the canopy and the Throne, Bernini uses the existing architecture in conjunction with his

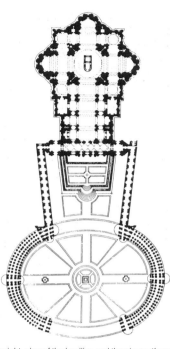

Above left, Apse pf S. Pietro showing part of the Baldacchino and the Chair of S. Pietro; right, plan of the basilica and the piazza (from Wittkower's «Arte e Architettura in Italia»); opposite page: 100 left, Scala Regia; below left, Equestrian statue of Constantine.

own inventions to exalt the traditional symbols of the church, expressed in the form of monumental sculpture, achieving the most spectacular theatrical effects. The **equestrian statue of Constantine** (1654-68) seems to be placed to the right of the portico of the basilica with the same grandiose yet elegant scenic result. Nearby stands another famous work by Bernini, part of the Vatican Palace, the **Scala Regia**, perhaps inspired by Borromini's **trompe l'oeil** in Palazzo Spada (no. 50); with a long narrow space available, the architect creates an optical illusion making the archway more imposing. The first columns are distanced from the wall, and further up they are actually shorter. Lastly, in 1656, Bernini received his final commission from Alexander VII Chigi to create the **Piazza** in front of the basilica. This piazza, which had to accommodate vast crowds for the pope's benediction, was conceived as an amphitheatre, elliptical in shape

(240 metres wide), it is far larger than the square area in front of the façade. It is surrounded by a free-standing Doric colonnade, consisting of 284 columns in rows of four supporting a continuous trabeation, surmounted by statues: this is a classical design, probably taken from Palladio, used on a gigantic scale in proportion to the dimensions of the basilica. As Wittkower observes, «When one crosses the piazza, the ever-changing perspective of the columns in their rows of four, seems to reveal a forest of individual shafts: the harmony of all these clearly-defined forms gives one a feeling of irresistible power. No other Italian building in the post-Renaissance period shows such a strong affinity with Greek architecture». Bernini wanted to complete the Piazza with a third colonnade on the eastern side, but this was never carried out.
[Piazza S. Pietro in Vaticano].

68

S. BIBIANA, Bernini, 1624-26. The early church of S. Bibiana (5th century) was rebuilt by Bernini in 1624: it is, thus, together with the baldacchino for S. Pietro, his first work as an architect. Over an open loggia with three bays, he designed a storey with three windows as though the building was a palazzo; the central part projects slightly, forming a square aedicule, the pediment of which dominates the side wings which end with a balustrade. The cornice of the wings seems to disappear beneath the pilasters of the aedicule, reappearing once more in the centre, thus creating a connecting link between the two parts of the building. This is a small building, with simple, clean lines, but full of elegance and originality. Inside, the statue of S. Bibiana on the high altar is also the work of Bernini, and is contemporary with the church; on the left-hand wall are frescoes by Pietro da Cortona from the same period. [Via Giolitti].

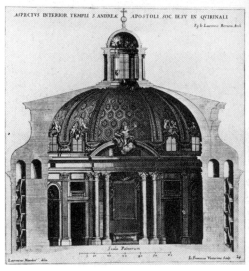

S. Andrea al Quirinale. Top left. Façade; top right. Section; immediately above, Plan of the church.

69

S. ANDREA AL QUIRINALE, Bernini, 1658-70.
The church of S. Andrea al Quirinale, commissioned in 1658 by Cardinal Camillo Pamphili, the nephew of Innocent X, for Jesuit novices, is considered to be Bernini's masterpiece. This, too, is a small church, with an oval ground plan, the entrance and presbytery being on the short sides. The façade resembles the central aedicule of S. Bibiana, with a semi-circular portico supported by two columns, inspired by S. Maria della Pace (no. 73). The trabeation of the portico continues the cornice line of the oval body of the church round the façade: the concave side walls emphasise the convex shape of the portico even further. Inside, the strong line of the trabeation echoes the motif of the exterior, curving in the iconostasis in front of the presbytery, on which stands the figure of S. Andrea. Thus, the basic plan of the construction is given emphasis, endowing this small building with dynamic energy and grandeur, typical of Bernini's architecture. Colour plays an important part in the interior: the rich tones of the polychrome marbles in the nave contrast with the white and gold stucco work of the dome.
[Via del Quirinale].

70

PALAZZO DI MONTECITORIO, Bernini / Fontana, 1650-94. Pope Innocent X Pamphili commissioned Bernini to design Palazzo Montecitorio in 1650: he intended giving it to the Ludovisi family. The work was almost completed when, in 1655, it was interrupted, and not continued until 1694 by Carlo Fontana. It was to house the papal tribunal; it is now the seat of the Italian Parliament. The architecture is on the whole traditional: its originality lies in the animated façade which is divided into five parts: a projecting central body, side wings which slant backwards, giving the whole façade a convex air: the end bays of the façade are projecting (there are 25 windows on each floor, 3-6-7-6-3). Each of these five parts is accentuated by giant pilasters which embrace the two upper storeys: the corner bays are decorated by rustication in imitation of natural rock - a motif inspired by the fashion for ruins of the period. This façade is almost entirely the work of Bernini: Fontana merely added the central entrance and the campanile above the clock. The palazzo became the home of the Italian Parliament in 1871: the elegant interior of the Chamber of Deputies in the Art Nouveau style of the turn of the century is the work of Ernesto Basile, 1918. In the centre of Piazza Montecitorio stands the obelisk of Psammeticus II which Augustus had brought from Egypt to be used as the gnomon for the sundial of Campus Martius, it once stood near Piazza S. Lorenzo in Licina.
[Piazza di Montecitorio].

71

PALAZZO CHIGI ODESCALCHI, Bernini, 1664. In 1664, before leaving for Paris where Louis XIV had summoned him to present his project for the Louvre, Bernini designed this palazzo for Cardinal Flavio Chigi. The façade has an original motif compared with traditional secular architecture (later much imitated both in Italy and abroad): for the first time above a smooth ground floor wall, there are two upper floors framed by gigantic composite pilasters. These pilasters are placed close together, almost touching the window frames, thus giving a marked rhythm to the façade. In the original project by Bernini, the central block had eight pilasters only, with a central doorway, and was flanked by two rusticated wings standing back. In 1745, the palazzo was acquired by the Odescalchi family who doubled its length, thus altering the original proportions. [Piazza SS. Apostoli].

Pietro da Cortona and Borromini. Pietro Berrettini, called **da Cortona** (1596-1669), worked as a painter in Florence before coming to Rome as a young man, where he soon acquired fame as both painter and architect, sponsored by the family of Pope Urban VIII Barberini. He painted the frescoes decorating the church of S. Bibiana (1624), Palazzo Barberini (1633), Palazzo Pitti in Florence (1646), S. Maria in Vallicella (1647-60) etc., in a highly dramatic style which owed something to Raffaello and the Venetian painters, and which was to have many imitators. His architecture, a synthesis of Renaissance classicism with elements of Tuscan Mannerism (Michelangelo), always shows originality. His first project was the Villa del Pigneto (near Rome) in 1625 (since destroyed), then the church of SS. Luca and Martina, the façade of S. Maria della Pace and the piazza in front of it, the façade of S. Maria in Via Lata, and lastly the great dome of S. Carlo al Corso (1668), one of the most beautiful in Rome; all these buildings are among the most successful expressions of Roman Baroque, together with the works of Bernini and Borromini. **Francesco Castelli, known as Borromini** (1599-1667), who was born near Lake Lugano, also came to Rome as a young man after having worked briefly in Milan, employed as stone-cutter, draughtsman and decorator on the building sites where his distant relative Carlo Maderno was working. He began to work as an independent architect rather late in life, unlike his contemporaries Bernini and Pietro da Cortona, the two other great architects of the period; however by this time he had acquired much practical experience both as builder and decorator. He was technically precise, with a difficult, introverted character, hard to please (he committed suicide finally), he was often given commissions for awkward sites, or to complete other architects' works (S. Agnese in Piazza Navona, the interior of S. Giovanni in Laterano and S. Andrea della Fratte). Wherever he was free to express his own ideas (S. Carlo alle Quattro Fontane, S. Ivo alla Sapienza, Collegio di Propaganda Fide), he let loose his extraordinary powers of inventiveness in a most original way: his buildings however, are always based in a precise geometrical scheme creating works of architecture that rival the complexity of Gothic masterpieces. His secular buildings are few and often incomplete, such as his work on Palazzo Spada (no. 50), or the façade of Palazzo Falconieri overlooking the Tiber. His disturbing, original buildings had an important influence much later, and especially in central Europe, e.g. late German Baroque.

72

SS. LUCA E MARTINA, Pietro da Cortona, 1635-50. In 1635 Cardinal Barberini commissioned Pietro da Cortona, who had made his name hitherto as a painter, to build the church of the Accademia di S. Luca, the guild of artists, on the site of the tomb of S. Martina (hence the double dedication). This is the first great Baroque church in Rome conceived and completed by the same architect. The façade in travertine is slightly convex with two orders both ending in horizontal architraves with the same curved motif; at either side double pilasters jut out so emphatically as to seem to squeeze the central wall, making it curve, as Wittkower noted. This contrast of rigid, angular elements with soft flowing curves is repeated both in the fine dome of this church and in the interior where the Greek cross plan is enlivened by a close succession of columns and pilasters without ornaments. In the upper part, instead, the pendants supporting the cupola and apse are covered with sumptuous stucco decoration. The fact that this interior is well-lit and completely white — there are no coloured marbles or frescoes — further emphasises the complex interplay of the architectural elements.
[Forum Romanum].

73

**S. MARIA DELLA PACE, Pietro da Cortona,
1656-57.** The church of S. Maria della Pace,
begun in 1482 and perhaps completed by
Bramante who also built the cloister (no. 44), was
restored by Pietro da Cortona in 1656: the Tuscan architect added the façade and laid out the
piazza in front of the church. The upper part of
the façade repeats the convex movement of the
Church of SS. Luca and Martina on a smaller
scale, and is strongly characterised by the semi-
circular portico, projecting between concave
wings; Bernini was to repeat this motif in his
Church of S. Andrea al Quirinale (no. 69). When
Pietro da Cortona laid out the small, irregularly-
shaped piazzetta round the front and sides of the
church, he treated the church as the stage and
the surrounding buildings as the auditorium of an
imaginary theatre. The elements he used are
classical, but the way in which they were
employed is typically Baroque.
[Piazza S. Maria della Pace].

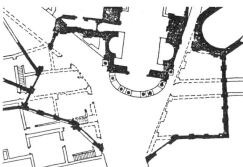

S. Maria della Pace. Top, Piazza S. Maria della Pace in a contemporary engraving: above right. Detail of the church façade;
below right, Plan of the square showing the former layout (from
Wittkower's «Arte e Architettura in Italia»).

Façade of S. Carlo.

74
S. MARIA IN VIA LATA, Pietro da Cortona, 1658-62. The ancient church of S. Maria in Via Lata (6th century) was rebuilt in the 15th century; Pietro da Cortona added the façade in 1658, giving the building a classical but severe simplicity. The façade consists of a portico and a loggia with four columns: the upper part has a Palladian window with a triangular gable. The central block juts forward from the side wings with their pilasters; the interior of the portico, with barrel vaulting supported by a double row of columns with side niches, is highly original.
[Via del Corso].

75
S. CARLO ALLE QUATTRO FONTANE, Borromini, 1638-67. The Spanish Trinitarians gave Borromini his first commission in 1634 to build a small convent by the Quattro Fontane; the site was narrow and awkward and Borromini began building the dormitory, refectory and cloisters: in 1638 he started work on the church which was completed in 1646. The façade was added in 1665-7, and is therefore one of the last works by Borromini. The ground plan of the church is more or less oval, even though the curved walls give an impression of great complexity: between the entrance, the apse and side chapels, columns are grouped in fours, while the high trabeation emphasises the movement of the walls and unifies the whole concept. The oval dome, supported by pendants, is lit both from the lantern and from the windows hidden behind the supporting cornice, thus emphasising the geometrical forms of the lacunar decoration. The façade is divided horizontally into two equally important

S. Carlo, interior.

Cloister; below, ground plan of the convent of S. Carlo.

areas, each with three bays divided by giant columns with smaller columns round the niches; the concave and convex cornices echo the undulating movement of the interior walls. The actual walls of the façade are almost eclipsed by the decorations: two cherubs frame the statue of S. Carlo Borromeo above the door. Borromini here does the opposite of Bernini who used architecture to highlight sculpture: in this case Borromini incorporates the sculpture within the structure, thus placing it at the service of the architecture. The highest praise for this first original work by Borromini was expressed by the Procurator General of the Spanish Order when he wrote «In the opinion of everybody, nothing similar as regards artistic merit, originality, excellence and singularity can be found anywhere in the world. Everything is ordered so that each part completes the next, and the spectator is invited to let his eyes run ceaselessly over the structure».
[Via del Quirinale].

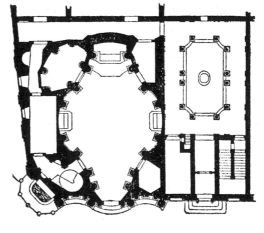

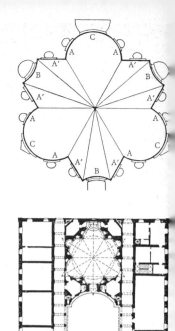

76

S. IVO ALLA SAPIENZA, Borromini, 1642-60.
The church of S. Ivo alla Sapienza was built by
Borromini at the end of the courtyard of the
Palazzo della Sapienza, designed by Giacomo
della Porta in 1587. It has a central ground plan,
in the form of a hexagon of 6 triangles, contained,
as it were, within a circle, with concave and convex walls. This variety of line was unified by giant
pilasters and by a high cornice, given great emphasis. The pilasters continue upwards in the
moulding of the dome: thus in the lower part of
the cupola the plan of the church is echoed, while
at the top, below the lantern, the form is circular,
making the vertical thrust almost awesome; in
this reduction from multiplicity to unity, from variety to the simplicity of the circle, lies much of the
fascination of this church: geometrical succinct-
ness and inexhaustible imagination, technical
skill and religious symbolism, have rarely found
such a reconciliation (Wittkower). The outside is
no less complex and original: the concave
façade in the courtyard echoes the motif of the
original portico; the many-sided convex tambour
of the cupola rises in the form of a cone to support
an elaborate lantern (built like the temple of Baal-
bek). The lantern is crowned by a soaring spiral
surmounted by a metal cusp. S. Ivo is not only
Borromini's masterpiece, but one of the most
daring constructions in the whole history of European architecture.
[Via della Sapienza].

Façade of the Oratory.

S. Ivo alla Sapienza. Opposite page: top right, Courtyard of the palazzo della Sapienza, at the far end the Borromini's church; top right, plan of the come and below, plan of the church (Wittkower's «Arte e Architettura in Italia»). This page: above, View of the dome; below, interior of the church.

77
ORATORIO DI S. FILIPPO NERI, Borromini, 1637-50. While Borromini was building the convent and church of S. Carlino, he also worked for the congregation of S. Filippo Neri, building the oratory adjoining their church of S. Maria in Vallicella or Chiesa Nuova (1575-1605). As well as the oratory he was commissioned to build a whole convent (refectory, library, cells, etc.); the façade — the most original part of the building — is slightly curved, divided into five spans by two orders of pilasters. In the centre there is a convex entrance and, above this, a window is set in a large niche: the building is crowned by a curved tympanum with a triangular point in the centre. In the lower order the simply-designed upper windows push upwards to touch the architrave: above, instead, the windows are set in an expanse of smooth wall, and framed by elaborate cornices. Although the façade is in brick, all the decorative elements are carried out elegantly with great attention to detail.
[Corso Vittorio Emanuele].

78

PALAZZO DI PROPAGANDA FIDE AND ORATORY, Borromini 1650-64. Borromini was working on the Palazzo di Propaganda Fide as early as 1650, however the façade in Via di Propaganda was completed between 1662 and 1664. It is divided into six bays by giant pilasters supporting a projecting entablature, above which is an important attic. The window above the door is convex, contrasting with the concave line of both the entablature, curving at that point, and the large side windows which, with their decorations, occupy all the space between pilasters. These contradictory curves of the façade and some anomalous features (the capitals of the pilasters are no more than grooves) convey a sense of disquiet and tension as do few other buildings by Borromini. The oratory inside the palazzo, dedicated to the Three Wise Men, is the last important religious building designed by Borromini, and took the place of Bernini's earlier oval construction (1634) which was smaller. The Borromini Oratory consists of a rectangular hall with rounded corners, full of light from its double row of windows. Giant pillars rise almost to the height of the architrave, but do not actually touch it: half way up there is a smaller order, above the entablature there is an uninterrupted row of large square windows. The pilasters, continuing beyond the architrave, become the ribs of the vault. «The coherent bone-structure has become of the greatest importance — there is hardly any wall between the tall pilasters!, and even the dome has been sacrificed for them... No other post-Renaissance building in Italy comes so near to Gothic principles. The Propaganda Fide church was a new, stimulating solution, and its cogent simplicity and persuasive logic are a fitting conclusion to Borromini's work in the field of church architecture» (Wittkower).

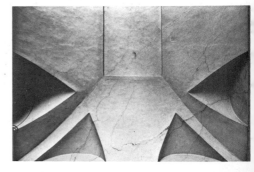

Opposite page: 10 left. Façade of the Propaganda Fide Palazzo; top right, interior of the oratory of the Re Magi. This page: above, details of the oratory, immediately above, Façade of the Palazzo.

S. Andrea della Fratte.

Close behind this building stands the church of **S. Andrea delle Fratte** in via Capo le Case, completed by Borromini in the same period. The church was begun in 1605 by Gaspare Guerra, and continued by Borromini from 1653 until 1665, but not completed. Borromini was responsible for the lantern of the dome and the bell tower at one corner. The tambour repeats with even greater emphasis the alternating concave and convex lines of the façade of S. Carlo; the bell tower close to the tambour is one of the most original inventions of Borromini, it might even be called bizarre. It has three orders, each one more complex than the one below: the base is square, above this rises a circular tower with columns like an ancient temple, surmounted by a balustrade (reminding us of Bramante's Tempietto); the third storey consists of pairs of figures supporting a complex cornice (similar to the lantern of S. Ivo's): above this are four volutes supporting a large vase, topped by a crown with spikes. This variety of ornamentation to the bell tower serves to emphasise the homogeneous curving mass of the tambour.

79
S. AGNESE IN PIAZZA NAVONA, Borromini, 1653-57.
Innocent X Pamphili's family palazzo overlooked Piazza Navona, and wishing to make the square more monumental, he commissioned Carlo Rainaldi to rebuild the old church of S. Agnese, adjoining the Pamphili palazzo. The pope, dissatisfied with the results, sacked Rainaldi and entrusted the work to Borromini. The church was already started with a Greek cross plan, and Borromini could do little to alter the interior of the main body of the church; however, he completely redesigned the dome and façade. The dome, with its very high tambour, is the tallest after that by Michelangelo, and really does dominate the façade, (in the way Michelangelo had conceived for St. Peter's) forming an integral part of the front of the church. The concave walls on either side of the entrance connect the side wings, with their tall ornate bell towers, to the central part. This church, with its perfect relationship between façade, dome and bell towers, was to have a strong influence on subsequent religious architecture.
[Piazza Navona].

Late Baroque. The most interesting figure in the second half of the 17th century was undoubtedly **Carlo Rainaldi** (1611-91); son of a well-known Roman architect, Girolamo, he worked with Domenico Fontana as a young man. Rainaldi's version of Baroque was more disciplined and classical, but always dynamic, as can be seen from his best works: the church of S. Maria in Campitelli, the churches in Piazza del Popolo (here we find a new concept of the piazza as the nodal centre for the urban scene), the apse of S. Maria Maggiore, the gardens of palazzo Borghese, etc. Another eminent architect, also from a family of builders, was **Martino Longhi the Younger** (1602-1660), best known for his elegant façade of the church of S. Vincenzo and Anastasio. Towards the end of the century, the architect most in demand was undoubtedly **Carlo Fontana** (1634-1714), nephew of Domenico Fontana (seventeenth-century architects seem to belong to dynasties). Fontana's success was due to the fact that he reduced Baroque architecture down to classical elements which were acceptable both to his patrons and to his numerous pupils, both Italian and foreign, some of whom were to become famous, e.g. Juvarra, Poppelmann in Germany, James Gibbs in England, etc. He inherited the post of architect of St. Peter's after Bernini, and was a tireless worker: among his works are the façade of S. Marcello, the Jesuit College at Loyola in Spain, the completion of Montecitorio, the churches of the Maddalena, S. Rita, S. Maria Assunta, and lastly the enormous Hospice of S. Michele (c. 1700), completed by Fuga (1735), one of the most interesting large buildings in Rome, now the Ministry of Cultural Affairs. Some works by **Antonio Gherardi** (1644-1702) should be mentioned on account of their essentially Baroque nature, such as the Avila chapel (1686) in S. Maria in Trastevere (no. 32).

80

SS. VINCENZO E ANASTASIO, Longhi the Younger, 1646-50. The façade of SS. Vincenzo e Anastasio, the parish church of the Quirinale, was built by Martino Longhi the Younger in 1646 for his patron Cardinal Mazzarino. Longhi came from a Lombard family of architects who had settled in Rome in the previous century. This is a typically Baroque construction, interesting on account of the groups of columns on either side of the main door and the window on the first floor. The fact that these columns stand away from the wall, a separation emphasised by the trabeation, gives the façade a vigorous, spectacular rhythm, an impression strengthened by the elaborate pediment crowning the building.
[Via S. Vincenzo].

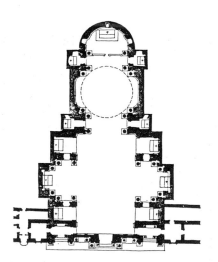

81

S. MARIA IN CAMPITELLI, Rainaldi, 1663-67.
S. Maria in Campitelli was built to house a
miraculous icon of the Madonna said to have
ended the plague in 1656: this explains the structure of the church, built by Carlo Rinaldi between
1663 and 1667. There are two parts to the
church, a nave on a Greek cross plan and a
square chapel with a dome where the image is
preserved; the interior has a theatrical effect,
thanks to the freestanding columns all round the
walls and the tall entablature, one's gaze being
drawn to the light from the chapel. The façade,
too, is of interest, with columns detached from
the wall, even more obviously than in the façade
of S. Vincenzo (no. 80); the pediments project
emphatically.
[Piazza Campitelli].

Piazza del Popolo. Above, Engraving by Piranesi: Nolli's plan of the Piazza (1748) before Valadier's work (1816-24). Overleaf: top left, View of the two 17th century curches.

82

THE 17th CENTURY CHURCHES IN PIAZZA DEL POPOLO, Rainaldi / Bernini, 1662-79.

The Porta Flaminia (no. 1) had always been the main entrance to the city from the north: from it Via del Corso follows the former route of the Via Flaminia (no. 2), leading to the Campidoglio (n. 54). In 1472 this entrance was given increased importance by the building of the church of S. Maria del Popolo (no. 43) under Pius IV (obelisk external façade of the gate, 1562) and Sixtus V (obelisk placed in the centre of the square by Domenico Fontana in 1589). In 1655, to celebrate the arrival in Rome of Queen Cristina of Sweden, who had been converted to Catholicism, Bernini decorated the inner façade of the Porta Flaminia in a sumptuous manner. Soon afterwards Pope Alexander VII Chigi decided to redesign the whole square: from which three important roads fanned out, leading to the centre of Rome: Via del Corso, Via Ripetta and Via del Babuino. The commission was given to Carlo Rainaldi in 1662: he planned two «twin» churches at the junction of these three roads, thereby increasing the spectacularly monumental setting of the square. The sites for the two

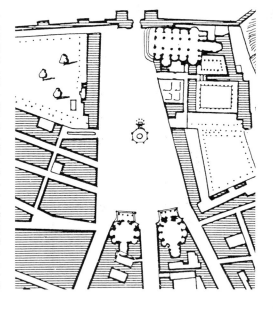

churches were, however, of different sizes: that on the left was narrower, therefore the church of **S. Maria di Montesanto** has an elliptical plan and an oval dome, while **S. Maria dei Miracoli** on the right, facing the churches, could be built with a circular plan and a perfectly hemispherical dome; each church has a classic pronaos of the same kind, thus both give the impression of being symmetrically identical, an impression aided by the presence of two bell towers on the side of Via del Corso. The work was interrupted and the plans altered by Bernini (1573-75) who modified the porticoes. In this way, Piazza del Popolo becomes the first example of an open square, different from the closed squares such as Campidoglio, S. Maria della Pace, S. Pietro; it is an urban area in which architecture and town planning are indivisible, a characteristic invention of the Baroque period which was to influence all modern town planning.
[c.f. no. 92).

83

S. MARCELLO, Carlo Fontana, 1682-83. S. Marcello is a very early church (perhaps 4th century), rebuilt after a fire by Jacopo Sansovino in 1519; the façade was added in 1682 by Carlo Fontana who here achieved one of his finest works. The façade is a typically late Baroque construction with the concave form and a wealth of decoration, whereas the clear symmetry of the architectural elements, columns and pilasters betrays classical trends of an academic nature which were then fashionable. It was this balanced mixture of classical and Baroque elements that made the façade of S. Marcello so admired and imitated.
[Via del Corso].

18th-19th CENTURY: FROM ROCOCO TO NEO-CLASSICISM

By the second half of the 17th century, Italy was no longer the artistic capital of Europe as it had been for the previous three centuries. Wealth, political power and culture became the monopoly of the countries of northern Europe: the new artistic capital of the continent was Paris. However, Italy (and Rome in particular) continued to attract artists from all over Europe, not because they hoped to find opportunities to work, but because they wanted to study the art of the past. During the 18th century, the significance of the architecture and of the world of the ancient Romans was rediscovered: this is the time of the Grand Tour of Europe. The first half of the 18th century saw much new building in Rome, however: some popes — Benedict XIII Orsini (1724-30), Clement XII Corsini (1730-40) and Benedict XIV Lambertini (1740-58) — undertook new constructions in the Baroque style in key points of the city. The first public museums were founded, especially for antiquities — the great passion of neo-classical culture: one of the greatest patrons of this movement was Clement XIII Rezzonico (1758-69) who appointed Winckelmann, the pioneer of modern archeology, as Director of Antiquities. During this papacy Piranesi built the church of the Priorato, and it is fitting that the monument to Clement XIII in S. Pietro was made by Antonio Canova, the famous neo-classical sculptor. In 1792, the Vatican Museum was opened to the public — one of the largest collections of ancient art in the world. The 19th century saw the end of the temporal power of the papacy; 10 years after the French Revolution, Pius VI was deported to France (1798), and Rome was proclaimed a republic. This republic was a very brief one: a year later, temporal power was re-established by Pius VI who had meanwhile been elected pope in Venice. In 1809, Napoleon made Rome part of his empire, nominating his son King of Rome. When the papacy was restored after the fall of Napoleon (1814), the papal states were re-established, even though reduced in size. The long papacy of Pius IX Mastai Ferretti (1846-78) was the last one to enjoy temporal power, and was particularly dramatic: in 1848, under the effect of the Risorgimento, Mazzini proclaimed the Roman Republic which, after only a few months, was suppressed by the French army. Finally the Franco-Prussian war of 1870 enabled the Kingdom of Italy, established 10 years earlier, to make Rome its new capital: the temporal power of the papacy was thus brought to an end after 14 centuries.

Rococo or Baroque. From 1820-40 a group of brilliant architects were working in Rome inspired by the almost-forgotten style of Borromini: they designed many buildings, including some of the most original and pleasing in the city. For the most part they are not great monuments but rather genial solutions to urban problems (e.g. the Porto di Ripetta, or the Spanish Steps in Piazza di Spagna), renewal of ancient basilicas, and, most numerous, palazzi and residential houses in a style halfway between Baroque and Rococo which was named «Barocchetto Romano». The architecture is simpler and more functional than that of the preceding period: the first middle-class houses to rent appeared on the market; some buildings heralded the later neo-classical movement. Among these architects were **Filippo Raguzzini** (1680-1771), Piazza S. Ignazio, Hospital and Church of S. Gallicano, S. Maria della Quercia; **Giuseppe Sardi** (1680-1753), Church of Maddalena and S. Pasquale; **Gabriele Valvassori** (1683-1761), Palazzo Doria Pamphili, S. Maria della Luce in Trastevere, houses near SS. Quirico and Giuditta; **Alessandro Specchi** (1668-1729), Porto di Ripetta, Palazzo de Carolis al Corso, Palazzo Spicchi; **Francesco De Sanctis** (1693-1740), the Spanish Steps, façade of Trinità dei Pellegrini; **Nicola Salvi** (1697-1751), Trevi Fountain (no. 101); **Ferdinando Fuga (1699-1781)**, Palazzo della Consulta, S. Maria dell'Orazione, façade of S. Maria Maggiore, palazzo Corsini; **Domenico Gregorini** (1700-1777), S. Croce in Gerusalemme. It should be noted that **Filippo Juvarra** (1678-1736) was in Rome from 1703-1714, assistant to Carlo Fontana, working mainly as a stage-designer; his only work of architecture in Rome is the Antamori chapel in the church of S. Girolamo della Carita. Finally **Alessandro Galilei** (1691-1736) designed the façade of S. Giovanni dei Fiorentini and that of S. Giovanni in Laterano (1735) in strict classical style. Thus ends the short but intense period of Rococo or «Barocchetto Romano».

84

SPANISH STEPS, De Sanctis, 1723-26. The Spanish steps form one of the most spectacular sights in Rome, together with the Campidoglio and Piazza del Popolo — all of which have incorporated uneven ground into the urban landscape with perfect ease. They are equidistant from Via del Corso and Porto di Ripetta, once the river port. These two points, Piazza di Spagna and Porto di Ripetta, were connected to the Porta Flaminia by Via del Babuino and Via di Ripetta, two of the three roads leading from Piazza del Popolo (no. 82) to the city centre with straight roads. Porto di Ripetta, with its wide curving staircase, was designed by Alessandro Specchi in 1704, and the Spanish Steps were built by Francesco de Sanctis in 1723. Previously, the Trinità dei Monti church was reached by wooded pathways up the hillside; the church was founded by Louis XII in 1502, completed by Giacomo della Porta in 1585, and restored (again by the French) in the early 19th century. Cardinal Mazzarino made an attempt to create a more monumental access to the French church, but it came to nothing. Soon afterwards, the French Chargé d'Affaires in Rome, Etienne Gueffier, died, leaving in his will a large sum for the construction of the steps; however they were not built until 60 years later. The choice of the architect was a good one: De Sanctis, with the Porto di Ripetta in mind, designed this sumptuously Baroque staircase. There are several ramps (a total of 138 steps) which curve, divide, meet up again with a series of four landings before reaching the church piazza. As Wölfflin remarks, «a Baroque conception, such as the Spanish Steps, can never be clearly perceived, even if it is observed many times, whereas a Renaissance work can be taken in at first glance; the Baroque will always have an air of mystery about it, even after the observer has memorised the design down to the last detail».

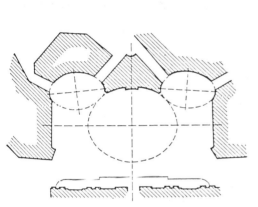

85

PIAZZA S. IGNAZIO, Raguzzini, 1726-27.
Another jewel of the «Barocchetto Romano»
style is the small square of S. Ignazio, designed
in 1726 by the Neapolitain architect Filippo
Raguzzini. He laid out the square in front of the
Church of S. Ignazio di Loyola, built 1626-50, attributed to Algardi. Raguzzini's project seems to
have been inspired by Pietro da Cortona's piazza
round the Church of S. Maria della Pace (no. 73):
here too residential houses surround an important church, but, in the case of S. Ignazio, the architect could not alter the church, and the surrounding houses were of a modest kind. Raguzzini, who was familiar with the work of Borromini,
reveals his small square to us gradually, from
several viewpoints. The complex design is based
on three oval shapes, the larger one in the centre
following the curve of the building, and the two
side ones are the concave ends of the two lateral
buildings.

86

PALAZZO DELLA CONSULTA, Fuga 1732-35.
The Palazzo della Consulta was built by Ferdinando Fuga in 1732-35 for the Tribunale della Santa Consulta (one of the papal courts) during the papacy of Clement XII. This elegant building is considered to be Fuga's masterpiece in the field of civic architecture: there is a subtle interplay of smooth pilasters alternating with the series of windows. The windows on the ground floor have small mezzanine openings immediately above them, while those on the first floor are surmounted by a large area of solid wall: under the roof line are tiny attic windows, above them an enphatic entablature, and lastly a delicate balustrade. The only decidedly Baroque element is the large coat of arms of Clement XII against the skyline, flanked by winged figures. [Piazza del Quirinale].

87

PALAZZO DORIA PAMPHILI, Valvassori 1730-35. Palazzo Doria Pamphili, built in the 15th century for the cardinals of the church of S. Maria in Via Lata (no. 74), was renovated (the wing giving onto the Via del Corso) by Gabriele Valvassori in 1730-35 for the Pamphili family; it later passed into the Doria family (it now houses the Doria Pamphili Gallery). This façade is typical of this period, full of originality, elegant and vigorous, with richly decorated pediments over the windows in the Rococo style; the windows, in groups of three, have balustrades running continuously along the first and second storeys, curving gracefully above the doorways. The windows on the ground and top floors seem to hang from the cornice dividing the floors, while those of the attic are linked by a frieze which continues along the façade. All the windows in this façade are given importance by the neutral wall of smooth rustication surrounding them. [Via del Corso].

88

TWO EARLY EIGHTEENTH-CENTURY CHURCHES: LA MADDALENA AND S. MARIA DELL'ORAZIONE. The churches of S. Maria Maddalena and S. Maria dell'Orazione e della Morte, both built in the centre of Rome during the 1730s, bear witness to the vitality and variety in Roman architecture in the early 18th century; when some architects showed a renewed interest in Borromini, while others tended to classical forms which were to become popular in the mid 18th century. The church of the **Maddalena**, in Via delle Colonelle near the Pantheon, was built in 1735 by **Giuseppe Sardi**, an original but little-known architect, who was the best Rococo designer in Rome, as Portoghesi noted. The façade is highly decorated, a series of convex and concave curves, inspired by S. Carlo (no. 75), divided by the emphatic cornices of the two orders. Inside, the elegant stucco decoration in the sacristy should be noted and the magnificent organ in the «Rocaille» style by the German organ-builder, J.C. Werle. The church of **S. Maria dell'Orazione e della Morte**, (1733-37), in Via Giulia close to Palazzo Farnese, belonged to the Confraternity of the same name whose task was to provide burial for the poor. It is the work of one of the most famous architects of the period in Rome, **Ferdinando Fuga** (façade of S. Maria Maggiore, no. 25, Palazzo della Consulta, no. 86, and Palazzo Corsini). Fuga followed the Baroque tradition of Maderno, Bernini and Borromini, but imposed a severe discipline on all the elements of the façade — a herald of the Neoclassical style. The oval interior with a cupola is interesting, inspired by S. Andrea al Quirinale (no. 69), but the oval here is placed lengthwise towards the altar; Fuga cleverly used the limited space available for four side chapels and a sacristy.

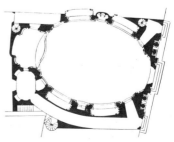

Top left. Façade of La Maddalena church; top right, Façade of S. Maria dell'Orazione; bottom right, Plan of S. Maria dell'Orazione.

89

S. CROCE IN GERUSALEMME, Gregorini and Passalacqua, 1742-44. Santa Croce in Gerusalemme, one of the seven basilicas which pilgrims to Rome had to visit, had been founded by Constantine, according to tradition, in one wing of his imperial palace to house the relics of the Cross which his mother St. Helen had carried from Jerusalem to Rome. The basilica was restored in 1144 (the bell tower dates from this rebuilding) and completely rebuilt in 1742 by Domenico Gregorini and Pietro Passalacqua, assistants of Filippo Juvarra. As Portoghesi observed, it can be considered the «swan-song of Baroque architecture in Rome». The façade curves in a delightfully Rococo manner, with its four groups of pilasters given great emphasis: it is crowned with a curving balustrade and statues. This Baroque construction contrasts with the contemporary façade of S. Giovanni in Laterano (no. 63) with classical forms, by Alessandro Galilei (1733-36). In S. Croce, the three entrances lead to an oval vestibule with a dome, surrounded by an ambulatory. The redesigning of the interior uses the same method that Borromini employed for S. Giovanni in Laterano: giant pilasters with a smaller order of granite columns. The baldacchino over the high altar is magnificently Baroque. [P. S. Croce in Gerusalemme].

Neo-classicism. Halfway through the 18th century, Rome became one of the capitals of Neo-classicism, the new style that was spreading rapidly all over Europe, on the wave of enthusiasm for the new archeological discoveries at Herculaneum (1738) and Pompei (1748). Classical architecture exemplified simple, severe forms which corresponded to the rationalist ideals of Enlightenment. One of the first and most influential theorists of this movement was the German writer **Johann Winckelmann** (1717-68), author of «The History of Ancient Art» (1764); he settled in Rome in 1755, and formed part of the group close to Cardinal Albani, and was then appointed Director of Antiquities of Rome by Clement XIII. Another member of the Albani circle was the German painter and writer **Anton Raphael Mengs** (1728-79), who decorated the Cardinal's villa and later became the official painter to the Spanish Court. During the period of the late 18th and the early 19th centuries, painters such as Ingres, Géricault, Kauffmann, Turner and Goya, and sculptors such as Houdon, Flaxman, Thorvaldsen and Canova came to Rome and lived there for long periods (Canova settled in Rome permanently from 1781 onwards). Of all the arts, architecture was most influenced by the rationalist ideals of Neo-classicism. Almost all the most famous architects of the time made pilgrimages to the sources of classical architecture to admire the ancient monuments: Soufflot from France, Adam, Dance and Soane from England, Schinkel from Germany, amongst many others. **Giovanni Battista Piranesi** (1720-1778), the Venetian engraver and architect who had settled in Rome in 1744, was the «seducer of all these young men», as Pevsner puts it; they had certainly been seduced before reaching Rome by Piranesi's visionary interpretations of ancient ruins, by this powerful romantic spirit, interpretations in which the artist «scales heaven with mountains of edifices» (Walpole). From this time, it could be said that Rome has almost always been seen through the eyes of this Venetian artist. Piranesi built little but that little was exquisite (not much was being built at this time). The most active architect in Rome was **Giuseppe Valadier** (1762-1839), he laid out the Piazza del Popolo and the Pincio and was responsible for the Valle theatre, the façades of S. Rocco and SS. Apostoli, the Palazzetto della Calcografia Nazionale, Porta al Ponte Milvio, Villa Torlonia on the Via Nomentana (with gardens by Jappelli), as well as various restorations of ancient monuments such as the Arch of Titus. The work of **Luigi Canina** (1795-1856) should not be forgotten, he worked on Villa Borghese and Porta del Popolo. An interesting industrial building in the final period of the papacy is the Manifattura Tabacchi (Tobacco Factory) in Trastevere (Sarti, 1863).

Villa Albani Torlonia. Top, Façade; immediately above, View of the Villa in an engraving by Piranesi; below right. One of the Tempietti at the end of the side wings.

90

VILLA ALBANI TORLONIA, Marchionni, 1743-63. Villa Albani, now Torlonia, was built by Carlo Marchionni between 1743 and 1763 for Cardinal Alessandro Albani, nephew of Clement XI, as a country villa near the Porta Salaria; it was designed to be not only a residence, but also a gallery for his large collection of ancient sculpture. It is a magnificent building, with two orders, a large portico on the ground floor but with no central feature. The two side wings are lower than the central part; this is a Palladian characteristic which helps to set the villa in its park, typical of this period of transition between late Baroque and a simpler, more classical kind of architecture — a prelude to Neo-classicism. The cultural environment in which Cardinal Albani played his part as patron of the arts was strictly Neo-classical: he had some of the most influential figures in the history of Neo-classicism in Europe as assistants and advisers: Winckelmann, archeologist and historian, and Mengs the painter, who decorated the vault of the gallery of Villa Albani with his famous fresco of Parnassus (1756-61), a real «manifesto» of Neo-classical painting.
[Via Salaria].

91

S. MARIA DEL PRIORATO, Piranesi, 1764-68.
In 1764, Cardinal Rezzonico, Prior of the Order of the Knights of Malta, commissioned Piranesi to rebuild the church of S. Maria del Priorato on the Aventine Hill. This is the first and only work of architecture of the Venetian artist, famous as an engraver of landscapes and archeological studies (he was to have worked on the rebuilding of the apse of S. Giovanni in Laterano, left unfinished by Borromini, but this was never carried out). Piranesi also laid out the delightful Piazza dei Cavalieri di Malta, decorating it with obelisks, small monuments and bas-reliefs, a fascinating scenic three-dimensional recreation of one of the artist's own engravings of ancient architecture. The façade of the church has a simple structure: a single order, four heavily grooved pilasters, an entrance door surmounted by an oculus and gable; the dense fabric of vertical elements cutting into the smooth wall with great precision. It almost seems to be one of his famous engravings of classical antiquities. The interior is on a Latin cross plan with side niches framed by giant pilasters, the ceiling decorated by stucco work: we are reminded of Borromini's interior of S. Giovanni in Laterano. The apse area, well lit, ends with a series of half columns recalling Palladio's presbytery of S. Giorgio Maggiore in Venice. The high altar is the most original part of the church: the upper part is a structure which resembles a boat on which rests a large smooth white sphere, supporting the figure of S. Basilio, surrounded by putti and clouds; the stucco work is by Tommaso Righi. The front of the altar is richly ornamented, while the back is perfectly plain, thus emphasising the complexity of its design. This interplay of contrasts between pure geometrical forms and the ancient fragment decoration is typically Neo-classical.
[Piazza dei Cavalieri di Malta].

S. Maria del Priorato. Top left, Façade of the church; top right, Deatil of the wall enclosing the square; below, Altar of S. Basilio.

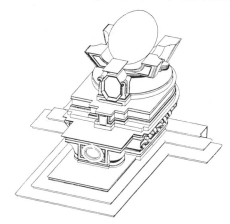

92

PIAZZA DEL POPOLO AND THE PINCIO, Valadier, 1816-24. In 1773 the Accademia di S. Luca held a competition to redesign the Piazza del Popolo (no. 83): in 1793 Giuseppe Valadier prepared his first plan for a trapezium-shaped piazza, then in 1810 he completed a very different project, this time for an elliptical-shaped piazza, which was carried out in 1816, making it the last important piece of town-planning on the part of the papal government of Rome, immediately after the fall of Napoleon. Piazza del Popolo, with the adjoining Pincio gardens along the ancient walls, is undoubtedly Valadier's masterpiece: his method was to respect existing monuments and the natural environment, emphasising both the artistic and the naturalistic elements, a synthesis of classicism and of respect for the landscape that is typically Neo-classical. Valadier's «Coffee House» (Casina Valadier) is particularly original in its simple elegance, standing on the highest point of the Pincio. Another typically Neo-classical feature, this time influenced by English landscape gardening, is the small lake, with the temple of Aescalapius in the middle, built in 1786 by Antonio Asprucci in the park of Villa Borghese (no. 64).

93

CAFFÈ GRECO, mid 19th century. Cafés have always been the meeting place for everyone, residents and visitors alike, places where the traveller and the tourist can sit down and feel at home, participating, even for a short time, in the daily life of the city: places like the Victorian pubs of London, the cafés of Saint-Germain-des Prés, Flore or Deux Magots, Florian's in Venice or the Caffé Greco in Rome. This café still has its typically Neo-classical décor, dating from the mid 19th century (the glass-covered rooms remind us of the galleries in Paris), with contemporary paintings on the walls — works by Angelica Kauffmann, Ippolito Caffi, etc. This elegant «drawing room» which is both Roman and international, and very much of the 19th century, is a delightful city monument (a Ministerial decree of 1953 gave official recognition to the fact), a good place to relax in after a tiring visit to the great monuments of Rome.
[Via Condotti].

THE CAPITAL OF ITALY

The last hundred years of the history of Rome — the history of the capital of a modern State — can be divided into three distinct periods: 50 years from 1871 to the First World War, with the growth of the new city capital; the period between the two world wars, 1918-45, which corresponds with the Fascist epoch, and, lastly, the 40-odd years of the post-war era up to the present day. These three periods were very different, yet all equally disastrous from an urban point of view. While it is true that the very end of the last century and the beginning of the present one were highly destructive in all the large European cities, London, Paris, Milan or Venice, in Rome the destruction was particularly ruthless. The city was adapted to its new rôle of capital with more energy than good taste, by destroying many fine buildings and building innumerable new ones, usually in the wrong places (the population doubled in two decades). These new constructions were acts of violence in the urban context, buildings out of scale, overdecorated, buildings that wanted to be important «pour épater les bourgeois», to satisfy politicians and the new class of bureaucrats which were beginning to form the majority of the city's inhabitants. The Fascist regime, at least in the historic centre of the city, caused more limited damage: it merely buried many of the remains of the Imperial Fora in order to build a motorway in the centre of the city. In the post-war period, Rome became the city with the largest number of inhabitants in Italy (almost 3 million): the green countryside round Rome disappeared under the cement of the sprawling suburbs, with no town plan, destroying that symbiosis that Rome has always enjoyed with the surrounding countryside. It is almost miraculous that this tough old city has not succumbed in face of all these adversities, but the spirit of old Rome seems to be indestructible.

The late 19th - early 20th centuries. Those large constructions in iron and glass, typical of the Industrial Revolution, are missing in Rome; also missing are the strange, original buildings of 19th century eclecticism, so visible in other European capitals (or if these buildings exist they have not yet been sufficiently studied and appreciated). There are very few examples of Ar Nouveau; instead this period produced the two most important and the ugliest constructions o the new capital of Italy, towering above the his toric centre like nightmares: the Palace of Justice (1889-1910) designed by **Guglielmo Calderini** this at least was useful to the city. The othe building is the Monument to Vittorio Emanuele II known as the Vittoriano (1885-1911), the work o **Giuseppe Sacconi**; with this construction two o the most ancient and glorious areas of the city were disfigured, the Campidoglio and Piazza Venezia. One of the best architects of the Ar Nouveau era, **Ernesto Basile** (1857-1932) worked in Rome for some time, but, apart from the interior of the Chamber of Deputies in Montecitorio (1918), he produced nothing else o note. To illustrate this period, works of two foreign architects have been chosen: Street from England and Hennebique from France — figures of great interest in the history of European architecture at the end of the last century. **George Street** (1824-81), a friend of Ruskin, was one o the most prolific and original exponents of neo-Gothic architecture during the second half of the century; William Morris and Philip Webb, the originators of the modern movement in architecture and in the applied arts, studied under Street. In fact, to decorate his church, Street chose Edward Burne-Jones, one of the foremost figures in William Morris' circle, the elegant English Pre-Raphaelite painter, specialist in glass work and mosaics. Street began another church in Rome, after S. Paolo: All Saints (1880), in Via del Babbuino, for the English Protestant community; it was completed after his death. **François Hennebique** (1843-1921), an engineer, was one of the first builders to use reinforced concrete on a large scale (others were François Coignet and Joseph Monier): in the hands of architects such as Perret and Le Corbusier, reinforced concrete was to become as noble a material as stone or brick, and in the post-war period in Rome it was to be used with great elegance by Pier Luigi Nervi and Riccardo Morandi.

Protestant church of S. Paolo. Above, Detail of Burne-Jones' mosaics; right, Façade and bell-tower of the church.

94

PROTESTANT CHURCH OF S. PAOLO, George Street, 1875-76. Between 1875 and 1876, George Street built the church of S. Paolo for the American Protestant community, in a central position on the Via Nazionale: it was one of his last works, but also one of his best, as Hitchcock observed. The style is Neo-gothic, used with great freedom. The bell tower seems to be a tribute to the Romanesque tradition in Rome, while the façade, decorated by alternate bands of stone and brickwork, points the way for future modern English architecture. The apse is decorated with mosaics by Burne-Jones. [Via Nazionale].

95

PONTE DEL RISORGIMENTO, Hennebique, 1910. This bridge was built for the Esposizione Universale, 1911, which was organised to celebrate the 50th anniversary of Italian unity; it is one of the most important works of François Hennebique, the pioneer of reinforced concrete. The bridge is a single span of reinforced concrete, 100 metres long and 20 metres wide, with a slender profile: here, function dictates the form, as in all good industrial design. After the ancient Roman bridges, this is the finest bridge over the Tiber, and heralds the constructions of Riccardo Morandi (no. 100).

Contemporary Architecture. During the twenties and thirties, the masters of modern architecture were at work throughout Europe and America — Perret, Le Corbusier, Gropius, Loos, Hoffmann Aalto, Wright, etc. — and unfortunately in this crucial period Italy was excluded from all this modern ferment. The fascist regime (1922-43) insisted on buildings in a mannered, classical style, allowing little experimental work, and thus preventing young architects from keeping up to date and from expressing themselves freely. The main exponent of the reactionary spirit of the regime is **Marcello Piacentini** (1881-1960) who was also responsible for two of the major urban projects of the thirties, the University City on the Via Tributina, and the EUR development. For these projects he enlisted the help of some of the most promising young architects of the period, such as **Giovanni Michelucci, Giuseppe Pagano** and **Gio Ponti**, but their contributions were suffocated by orders that came from above, and can hardly be discerned. An exception is the Fencing Gymnasium of the Foro Italico, a masterpiece by **Luigi Moretti**. In contrast, Italian architecture in the post-war period was a revelation on the international scene: «Architecture in Italy today has a vitality, an exuberance and a personality which makes it fascinating and unique. However, Italy is capable of producing more architectural horrors than any other European country, while its land usage is almost unrelievedly shocking». This lapidary definition of the state of Italian architecture was made in 1961 by an acute American critic, Kidder Smith, and unfortunately it is still true today. Examples of good, even excellent, modern architecture are certainly not lacking in Rome, even though they are not as numerous as in other cities, such as Milan, for example. Worthy of mention are the Rinascente (1957-61) by **Franco Albini** and **Franca Helg**, various private houses by **Mario Ridolfi**, who with **Ludovico Quaroni** was responsible for the Quartiere Tiburtino project, **Luigi Moretti**, the **Passarelli** group, **Carlo Aymonimo**, and others. The last items have been chosen as examples of town planning which take into account human values (Quartiere Tiburtino) such as urban structures, the Termini train station, sports facilities designed by **Pier Luigi Nervi**, buildings by **Riccardo Morandi**, and finally, a monument, the Fosse Ardeatine, expression of a society which needs landmarks for its own historical memories.

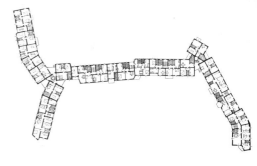

96

INA HOUSING IN THE TIBURTINO DISTRICT, Quaroni / Ridolfi, 1949-54. This project for low-cost housing in the Tiburtino district was carried out between 1949-54 by a group of architects under Ludovico Quaroni and Mario Ridolfi: it is one of the very few examples, not only in Rome but in the whole of Italy, of a well-designed, low-cost housing project comparable to the best European tradition. The overall plan of the area, which takes the lie of the land into consideration, combined with simple but distinguished architecture, results in high-density housing without recourse to high-rise blocks. The whole project has been described as 'neo-realist', but it is an honest attempt to avoid the desperate suburban squalor of almost all large modern cities, and rediscover the scale of the pre-modern city which developed gradually over a long period of time. Good architecture must be combined with good town planning, otherwise the results are, at best, either cathedrals in the desert or utopias that are only viable on the drawing board.

97

TERMINI TRAIN STATION, Montuori, Calini, Castellazzi, Fadigati, Vitellozzi, Pintonello, 1948-50. The Termini train station was begun just before the war and completed, from 1948-50, by the architects Montuori, Calini, Castellazzi, Fadigati, Vitellozzi and Pintonello. The solution of the projecting roof is brilliant: in front of the great concourse (128 metres wide), the roof curves in harmony with the Servian Walls (no. 1) remains of which stand majestically immediately to the side of the station building, almost a part of the design; the city of Rome could not have a more exciting entrance. The curved roof connects the concourse and the platforms in a functional way, creating fluid, well-lit spaces; glass walls, recourse to metal structures, well-defined details all help to make up «the finest train station in Europe», as it has been acclaimed by architectural critics.
[Piazza del Cinquecento].

98

FOSSE ARDEATINE, Aprile, Calcaprina, Cardelli, Fiorentino, Perugini, 1949. In the Via Ardeatina, parallel to the Via Appia Antica, and not far from the basilica of S. Sebastiano and the tomb of Cecilia Metella, stands the Monument of the Fosse Ardeatine, built to commemorate the massacre of 335 innocent Italians by the German troops as retaliation for the ambush in Via Rasella on May 24th 1944. The civilians, who had nothing to do with the ambush, but were chosen at random, were taken to the quarries in this area and shot, then the entrance to the quarries was blown up to hide the bodies. The architects have left the area intact, and covered it with a reinforced cement structure, a sort of enormous sarcophagus, supported by six pillars; beneath this roof are 335 identical tombs. It is an unadorned, severe monument, and all the more impressive and moving for this reason. It was designed by the architects Aprile, Calcaprina, Cardelli, Fiorentino and Perugini. The bronze gates are by Mirko Balsaldella.
[Via Ardeatina, Via Appia Antica].

Palazzetto dello Sport (detail), 1960.

Flaminio Stadium, 1960.

Palazzetto dello Sport.

99
NERVI'S OLYMPIC SPORTS FACILITIES, 1959-60. Pier Luigi Nervi built three important sports facilities for the 1960 Olympic Games in Rome, the Palazzo dello Sport in the EUR, the **Palazzetto dello Sport** and the **Flaminio stadium** in Via Flaminia, close to the Olympic village. The Palazzo dello Sport in the EUR is the largest structure: a dome, diameter 100 metres, like an upturned bowl, covers space for 15,000 spectators; from the outside it is impossible to appreciate the elegance of the vast cement structure through the glass walls. The Palazzetto, another circular arena, is much smaller (room for 5,000 spectators), but far more interesting as a piece of architecture; the dome is 58.5 metres in diameter, supported by 36 Y-shaped pylons, leaning in line with the curve of the dome, giving the construction a feeling of tension and lightness (consisting of 1,620 prefabricated elements of reinforced concrete). In 1971 Nervi built the Audience Hall in the Vatican able to accommodate 12,000 spectators, with a shell-shaped vaulted ceiling.

Fly-over bridge crossing the via Olimpica, 1960.

Bridge over the Tiber at Magliana, 1967.

Boeing hangar, 1970.

100

BUILDINGS BY RICCARDO MORANDI, 1958-70. «Even a superficial knowledge of design tells us that it is always possibile, within certain limits, to provide several solutions similar functionally, statically and economically. At this point the choice of the solution and the careful attention to formal details (this is almost always independent from the requirements of the calculations) transcend the merely technical level and, consciously or unconsciously, become artistic creation». This straightforward declaration by Riccardo Morandi ought to be displayed, written large, in all central and regional offices of the Ministry of Works, as well as in the offices of building departments of all Italian cities. Modern architecture, especially public building, will only have a future worthy of its past if it follows the example of the best of our contemporary architects, and here must be included two great figures from the Roman school, Ludovico Quaroni and Riccardo Morandi, not only because of the high quality of their work in all their different types of projects, but because of the method with which they deal with some fundamental problems that face architects today. Riccardo Morandi, «the most valid, original structuralist in Italy» (Tafuri), one of the foremost on

the international scene, has shown that it is possible to transform the concept of utilitarian structure into architectural expression without being gratuitously spectacular (as Nervi has sometimes done, unfortunately), using the minimum effort for the maximum result. He was born in Rome in 1902 and spent his life there, but built little in his native city — more proof of the shortsightedness of public commissions in Italy. His works in Rome are exemplary: the slender viaduct **Cavalcavia over the Via Olimpica** in Corso Francia (1958-59), the **Bridge over the Tiber at the Magliana** on the Rome-Fiumicino motorway, a complex, tensile construction, (1965-67), a very difficult operation because of the conditions of the terrain, and lastly, work on the **Leonardo da Vinci Airport of Rome** at Fiumicino (terminals, underground car parks, entrance viaduct, etc.); special mention should be made of the enormous **Alitalia hangars** (1961-62) and the **Boeing Maintenance Centre** (1969-70) supported by cables, each covering an area of 10,000 square metres: for lightness, strength and elegance these structures can only be compared to the creations of Gustave Eiffel.

Fountain in front of the Pantheon, 1575.

Fountain of the Tortoises, Landini, 1584.

101

THE FOUNTAINS OF ROME. The fountains of Rome are perhaps the most precious bequest left to the modern city by the building skill of the ancient Romans. These fountains were, for the most part, built between the 15th and the 17th centuries, using the aqueduct structures which the Romans had built fifteen centuries earlier (c.f. no. 3): these were not replaced until the late 19th century. In 1475 Pope Sixtus IV della Rovere restored the Acquedotto dell'Acqua Vergine, planned by Agrippa (25-20 B.C.) to supply the baths in Campus Martius. Originally these aqueducts brought water to the Trevi Fountain (the magnificent sculptures were added in the 18th century), but were used for almost all the other fountains in the Via del Corso area. One century later, Sixtus V brought into use again a branch of the Aqua Marcia aqueduct which had supplied the baths of Diocletian (298-305, A.D.), the Marcia Jovia, later known as Aqua Felice after the name of Pope Felice Peretti, to bring water to the Termini and the Quirinal areas. Soon afterwards, Paul V Borghese, who had started to replan Trastevere, restored the Traiano aqueduct (1st-2nd centuries A.D.) and, by means of the Aqua Alsietina source, supplied water to the whole of the Gianicolo quarter. The earliest fountains still

functioning today are built by Gregory XIII Boncompagni about 1575, designed by Giacomo della Porta, those playing in the Piazza del Popolo, in front of the Pantheon, Piazza Colonna, Piazza Navona, etc., always using the Aqua Vergine supply. One of the most famous of these is the fountain in front of the **Pantheon** in Piazza della Rotonda: a quadrilobate basin with an Egyptian obelisk in the centre (placed there in 1711). The most elegant of these 16th century fountains, **Fontana delle Tartarughe** (1581-84) in Piazza Mattei, decorated with boys playing with dolphins with one hand and holding tortoises up to drink in the top basin with the other (the tortoises were added in the 17th century). This elegant Mannerist work of art was designed by Taddeo Landini. The imposing, but rather heavy, **Fontana Felice** (also known as Moses) was designed by Domenico Fontana for Sixtus V in 1585: it stands in Piazza S. Bernardo; Fontana also designed the fountain in **Piazza del Quirinale** in 1588. The same pope commissioned the **Quattro Fontane** for the intersection between Strada Pia and Strada Felice (now called Via delle Quattro Fontane): each corner of the cross roads is decorated with a different statue, two of river gods, the

«Felice» Fountain, by Domenico Fontana, 1585.

Fountain in front of the Quirinale, by Domenico Fontana, 1588.

Tiber and the Nile, and two pagan divinities, Juno and Diana. Paul V Borghese, another great builder of fountains, following the example of his predecessor, commissioned the **Fontana Paola** (1610) on the Gianicolo, later in 1613 he appointed Carlo Maderno to design the fountains of **Piazza S. Pietro** and **Piazza S. Maria Maggiore**. In 1627 the great Bernini began to design fountains: his earliest attempt is rather modest, the **Barcaccia** in Piazza di Spagna (it may have been the work of his father, Pietro), taking an ancient theme (already used in 1513 for the fountain of the Navicella in front of S. Maria in Domnica, perhaps the implication is that the church is like a ship), but adding an original note: he lowers the edge of the basin to show off the sculpture and to reveal the movement of the water. His masterpiece in fountain design is undoubtedly the **Fontana dei Quattro Fiumi** in Piazza Navona. Here, in 1575, Giacomo della Porta had designed the fountains at either end of the piazza (they were subsequently altered); Bernini was commissioned in 1651 to design the central fountain in the piazza which had to include the obelisk from the Circus of Maxentius as its main decorative element. Bernini placed the obelisk on top of a grandiose rock formation containing a grotto

and at the four corners personifications of rivers (these sculptures were carried out by Bernini's assistants according to his design), Danube, Nile, Ganges and Rio della Plata, symbolising the four continents. The total effect of the powerful sculptures, the rocks and the flowing water is astonishing, rather like a stage scene. Bernini also designed the **Fontana del Tritone** in Piazza Barberini in 1641: here the sculptural element is foremost; Triton, seated on a scallop shell which is supported by four dolphins, is blowing a conch shell from which water spouts. The **Fontana di Trevi**, the most magnificent and also the earliest fountain in Rome, was designed by Nicola Salvi (1732-62). The central figure of Ocean dominates the scene from his shell-shaped coach, pulled by two seahorses, led by tritons, all against the background of a triumphal arch, enlivened by the tumultuous cascade of water. On the left, the statue of Abundance and that of Health to the right in niches, and above them, bas-reliefs showing Agrippa commanding the aqueduct to be built, and the discovery of the source by the Virgin who gave her name to the aqueduct. In this fountain, Salvi puts to good use all he had learned from Bernini, creating the most spectacular fountain ever seen in a city, before or

133

Paola Fountain, 1612.

Fountain in Piazza S. Pietro, Maderno, 1613.

One of the Quattro Fontane, 1593.

Triton Fountain in Piazza Barberini, Bernini, 1641.

Fountain of the Rivers, Piazza Navona, Bernini, 1651.

Barcaccia Fountain, Piazza di Spagna, Bernini, 1627.

Trevi Fountain, Salvi, 1762.

since. Some more recent fountains are worthy of note: that of Valadier in the Piazza del Popolo (1822), and the Fontana della Naiadi in Piazza Esedra with its graceful Art Nouveau figures sculptures by Mario Rutelli (1912). Water, sculpture, architecture and vegetation combine in sumptuous Baroque concepts in the splendid gardens of the villas in the Roman countryside, Tivoli or Frascati. The memory of the music of fountains playing is an integral part of a visit to Rome, and for this we must thank the hydraulic engineers of ancient Rome who understood the secrets of conveying water to the city.

Fountains in the 17th century gardens of Villa d'Este at Tivoli.

From left to right: Fencing School, L. Moretti (1934-36); La Rinascente, Albini/Helg (1957-61); Shops and flats in Via Campania, Studio Passarelli (1963-65).

A FURTHER SELECTION OF BUILDINGS
Buildings marked thus (*) are of particular interest.

Ancient buildings

* Circo Massimo, II c. B.C. - II c. A.D., Parco del Circo Massimo
* Tomb of the Scipioni, II c. B.C., Via di Porta S. Sebastiano
- Bath of Agrippa, I c. B.C., Via dell'Arco della Ciambella
- Cloaca Massima, II c. B.C., Piazza Bocca della Verità
- Temple of Apollo Sosiano, I c. B.C., near Teatro Marcello (see no. 18)
* Portico di Ottavia, I c. B.C., Via del Portico di Ottavia
* Temple of Venus and Rome, I c. A.D., near Colosseo (see no. 19)
* Basilica of Porta Maggiore, I c. A.D., Via Prenestina (see no. 1)
- Tomb of Virgilio Eurisace, I c. A.D., Porta Maggiore
- Castro Pretorio, I c. A.D., Viale del Policlinico
- Temple of Hadrian (Borsa), II c., Piazza di Pietra
* Catacomb of Priscilla, II c., Via Salaria
* Catacomb of S. Callisto, III c., Via Appia
* Mithraic temple, II-III c., Via S. Prisca
* Amphitheatre Castrense, III c., Piazza S. Croce in Gerusalemme
- Arch of the Argentari, III c., Piazza Bocca della Verità

Early Christian and Medieval buildings

* S. Maria Antiqua, VI-VIII c., Roman Forum
* SS. Cosma e Damiano, VI c., Foro Romano (see no. 4)
- S. Balbina, VI-VII c., Viale G. Baccelli
- S. Giorgio in Velabro, VI-VII c. Via del Velabro
- Leonine Walls, IX c., Vaticano

- SS. Nereo e Aquileo, IX c., Via di Porta S. Sebastiano
* SS. Giovanni e Paolo, XI-XII c., Piazza SS. Giovanni e Paolo
* SS. Quattro Coronati, XII c., Via dei Santi Quattro Coronati
- Anguillara Tower, XIII c., Piazza S. Sonnino
- Tower of the Conti, XIII c., Largo Ricci
- Tower of the Capocci, XIII c., Piazza S. Martino ai Monti

Renaissance (15th - 16th Century)

- S. Pietro in Vincoli, B. Pontelli (?), 1471-1503, Piazza S. Pietro in Vincoli
* S. Pietro in Montorio, B. Pontelli (?), 1472-1500, Via Garibaldi (see no. 45)
* Sistine Chapel, 1475-81, B. Pontelli, Vaticano
- S. Agostino, Giacomo da Pietrasanta, 1479-83, Piazza S. Agostino
- S. Maria di Monserrato, Ant. da Sangallo il V., façade XVI c., Via Monserrato
- S. Maria dell'Anima, Giul. da Sangallo (?), 1500-23, Via S. Maria dell'Anima
* S. Giovanni dei Fiorentini, Jacopo Sansovino, early XVI c., completed by Giac. Della Porta / C. Maderno 1614, façade by A. Galilei, 1734, Via Giulia
* S. Spirito in Sassia, Ant. da Sangallo il G., 1540, Borgo S. Spirito
* S. Caterina dei Funari, G. Guidetti, 1560-64, Via dei Funari
- S. Maria dell'Orto, G. Guidetti (?), 1566, façade attr. Vignola, Via S. Maria dell'Orto
* S. Luigi dei Francesi, D. Fontana, façade G. Della Porta, 1580-89, Piazza S. Luigi dei Francesi
- S. Maria in Vallicella or Chiesa Nuova, M. Longhi il V., 1583-1605, Piazza della Chiesa Nuova (see no. 77)

- S. Bernardo alle Terme, 1598, Piazza S. Bernardo (see no. 65)
- House of Cavalieri di Malta, 1467-70, Piazzetta del Grillo
- House of Cardinale Bessarione, XV c., Via di Porta S. Sebastiano
* Ospedale di S. Spirito, 1473-78, Borgo S. Spirito
- Albergo dell'Orso, XV c., Via dell'Orso
- Palazzo Regis (Piccola Farnesina), A. da Sangallo il G. (?), 1523, Corso Vitt. Emanuele
- Palazzo Sachetti, Ant. da Sangallo il G., 1543, Via Giulia
* Palazzo Ruspoli-Caetani, B. Ammannati, 1556, Via del Corso
- Palazzo Firenze, XV c., courtyard B. Ammannati, Piazza Firenze
* Palazzo Ricci-Peracciani, Nanni di Baccio (?), 1550, Piazza Ricci
- Gate of Villa Farnese, Vignola (?), 1565-73, Palatino (see no. 6)
* Palazzo della Sapienza, G. della Porta, 1587, Corso Rinascimento (see no. 76)
- Palazzetto Zuccaro, F. Zuccaro, XVI c., Via Sistina

17th Century

- S. Sebastiano, F. Ponzio / G. Vasanzio, 1608-13, Via Appia
* S. Carlo al Corso, O. e M. Longhi il G., 1612; dome P. da Cortona, 1668, Via del Corso
* S. Carlo ai Catinari, R. Rosati, façade G.B. Soria, 1612-38, Piazza Cairoli
* S. Andrea della Valle, G. Della Porta / C. Maderno / C. Rainaldi; dome C. Maderno, 1591-1665, Corso V. Emanuele
- S. Ignazio di Loyola, O. Grassi / C. Maderno, 1626-50, Piazza S. Ignazio (see no. 85)
* S. Gregorio Magno, G.B. Soria, 1629-33, Via S. Gregorio Magno
* S. Maria dei Sette Dolori, F. Borromini, 1650, Via Garibaldi
* Cappella Spada, F. Borromini, 1660, Church of S. Girolamo, Via di Monserrato
- Oratorio di S. Giovanni in Oleo, F. Borromini, 1658, Via Latina
- Chiesa di Gesù e Maria, C. Rainaldi, 1670-75, Via del Corso
- S. Rocco, G.A. De Rossi, 1657; façade G. Valadier, 1834, Via Tomacelli
- S. Pantaleo, G.A. De Rossi, 1681-89, façade G. Valadier, 1805, Piazza S. Pantaleo
- S. Antonio dei Portoghesi, M. Longhi il G. / C. Rainaldi, end 16th c., Via dei Portoghesi
- S. Girolamo della Carità, C. Rainaldi, 1660, Via Monserrato
- Casino dell'Aurora (ex Villa Ludovisi), c. 1620, Via Aurora
- Palazzo Pallavicini Rospigliosi, G. Vasanzio / C. Maderno, 1611-16, Via XXIV Maggio
* Palazzo Falconieri, F. Borromini, 1640, Via Giulia
- Palazzo di Spagna, staircase, F. Borromini, 1640, Piazza di Spagna

- Palazzo Carpegna, staircase, F. Borromini, 1643, Via della Stampella
* Palazzo Pamphili, C. Rainaldi, 1644-50, Piazza Navona (see no. 79)
* Villa Pamphili, A. Algardi / C. Rainaldi (?), 1645-47, Via S. Pancrazio
- Palazzo Madama (Senate House), façade L. Carli / P. Marucelli, 1649, Corso Rinascimento
- Palazzo Chigi, G. Della Porta 1580, completed by C. Maderno / F. Della Greca, 1660, Via del Corso
- Palazzo Pio, C. Arcucci, 1650, Piazza Campo dei Fiori

18th - 19th Century

- SS. Apostoli, C. Fontana, 1702-14, Piazza SS. Apostoli
* Cappella Antamoro, F. Juvarra, 1708, Church of S. Girolamo
- Trinità dei Pellegrini, façade F. De Sanctis, 1723, Piazza dei Pellegrini
* S. Maria della Quercia, F. Raguzzini, 1725, Piazza della Quercia
- SS. Nome di Maria, A. Deriset, 1738, Foro Traiano (see. nos. 5 and 55)
- S. Apollinare, F. Fuga, 1742-8, Piazza S. Apollinare
- S. Pasquale Baylon, G. Sardi, 1745, Via delle Fratte di Trastevere
- Palazzo Roccagiovine, A. Specchi, 1710, Piazza Farnese
- Palazzo De Carolis, A. Specchi, 1720 c., Via del Corso
* Ospedale S. Gallicano, F. Raguzzini, 1725, Viale Trastevere
* Ospizio S. Michele, C. Fontana / F. Fuga, 1693-1790, Via S. Michele
- Palazzo Corsini, F. Fuga, 1729-32, Via della Lungara
- Palazzo Doria, P. Ameli, 1743, Via del Plebiscito (see no. 87)
- Villa Torlonia, G. Valadier / G.B. Caretti, garden G. Japelli, 1806-40, Via Nomentana
- Teatro Valle, G. Valadier, 1819-22, Via del Teatro Valle
- Teatro Argentina, P. Camporese, 1837, Via Torre Argentina
- Gate of Villa Borghese, L. Canina, 1825, Piazzale Flaminio

The Italian Capital

- Museo Geologico, Ing. Canevari, 1875, Largo S. Susanna
- Galleria Sciarra, G. De Angelis, 1890, Via Minghetti
- Synagogue, L. Costa / O. Armanni, 1889, Ghetto
- Piazza Esedra, G. Koch, 1896 (see no. 21)
- Villa Ximenes, E. Basile, 1918, Piazza Galeno
* University City, planning, M. Piacentini: Istituto di Fisica, G. Pagano; Facoltà di Matematica, G. Ponti; Istituto di Mineralogia, G. Michelucci, 1932-35

* Eur, planning M. Piacentini, 1935-41
* Palestra per la Scherma, L. Moretti, 1934-36, Viale delle Olimpiadi
- Casa del Girasole, L. Moretti, 1947-50, Via B. Buozzi 64
* La Rinascente, Albini / Helg, 1957-61, Piazza Fiume
- Olympic Village, Cafiero / Libera / Luccichenti / Moretti / Monaco, 1957-60 (see nos. 99-100)
- Incis Housing, planning, L. Moretti, 1960-63, Via Sabatini
- British Embassy, Sir Basil Spence, 1960-71, Via XX Settembre 64
- Office Building, L. Moretti / V. Morpurgo, 1961-65, Piazzale dell'Industria, Eur
- Housing, C. Aymonino / A. De Rossi / C. Chiari, 1962-63, Via Agnani n. 93-101
* Shops and flats, Studio Passarelli, 1963-5, Via Campania
- Hostel S. Tommaso, Studio Passarelli, 1963 Via degli Ibernesi 20
- Collegio Latino Americano, J. Lafuente / Studio Passarelli, 1965, Via Aurelia Antica 408
- Casa Papanice, P. Portoghesi / G. Gigliotti, 1966-70, Via G. Marchi 1
- Corviale Housing, M. Fiorentino / R. Morandi 1972-82, Via Portuense
* Mosque and Islamic Centre, P. Portoghesi / V. Gigliotti / S. Moussawi, 1975-90, Via G. Pezzana
- Esso Offices, J. Lafuente / G. Rebecchini, 1977-80, Viale del Castello della Magliana
* IBM Buildings, M. Zanuso / P. Crescini, 1979-82, Via Ardeatina

Index

Figures refer to item numbers

Acknowledgements

Photographs are by *Michel Regnault de la Mothe, Venice,* excluding:

Fondazione Cini, Venice: page 11, 20, 23, 24, nos. 3, 15, 54, 62, 82, 90.

Istituto Centrale per il Catalogo e la Documentazione, Rome, page 8, nos. 42, 46, 57, 71, 90.

Guido Lion, Venice, page 32.

Riccardo Morandi, Rome, no. 100.

Oscar Savio, Rome: page 10, 28, nos. 22, 28, 30, 32, 47, 49, 50, 63, 71, 72, 80, 81, 83, 93, 98.

Drawings, if not stated otherwise, are by *Marco Regnault de la Mothe, Venice.*